RIDDLES FOR SMART KIDS

Riddles for Smart Kids

Riddles and trick questions for kids to enjoy with the whole family. Fun brain busters for ages 4-12

The Riddle Academy

CONTENTS

3
HARD RIDDLES

4

BONUS

1

INTRODUCTION

We are living in a world where everything is revolving around social media. As such, it has become exceedingly difficult for adults to find exciting ways for children to learn outside such platforms. Riddles are important because they allow parents to bond with their children as well as expose them to a wide range of knowledge. Riddles have more extra importance on the mental health of kids than most parents imagine. It is, therefore, important for parents to spend time with their children sharing riddles and explaining all the logic behind every riddle you get to crack. One of the greatest ways to help a child release stress after struggling with paying attention after hours of stillness is by sharing a riddle. This is because riddles introduce intellectual humor to such kids, take away the stress they might have as well as give them a new concentration span. Also, the intellectual humor takes away boredom, thus the importance of introducing a riddle to kids in mid-class.

Riddles help in child brain development as they assist children in learning problem-solving techniques and skills in critical thinking very early in life. Children can also pick up the vocabulary skill from riddles since they will always look forward to having fun cracking exciting riddles. Riddles come in handy for antisocial children too. This is because they involve asking tricky questions between friends in a social setting. Therefore, a child who is shy of talking in front of many people can be encouraged to be confident and social by having a session where they share riddles amongst themselves. Kids also love riddles because they can use them to show off their learned skills. This is great because it makes them want to learn more and more riddles.

There are various topics that a child can learn from the different riddles. Therefore, it is important for every adult who understands the importance of riddles to ensure that they expose their children to as many riddles as possible. Riddles can be repeated severally and still be fun for kids. When riddles are repeated to kids many times and they are allowed to share the ones they are familiar, it will enhance their understanding. There are so many riddles available depending on the occasion, age gap and interests of your child.

Finding riddles on topics that your child likes will make him or her more entertained and make it easy for them to learn. As an adult, give a child a chance to tell you the riddles they like and also assist them in finding the answers to any hard riddles they might have come across. Adults should also keep in mind that, as much as kids think riddles are meant for fun, they normally get the positively intended messages behind the riddles. Every time after a riddle is told, go through it with the child and bring out the real message behind the riddle together.

1

RIDDLES FOR KIDS AGES 4-8

2

FUN RIDDLES

Animals Riddles:

1. If you've ever been to the zoo, you've seen a bear. If you've seen old pictures, you know they are in black and white. The animal I'm describing looks like it's stuck in one of Grandpa's old pics.
2. What do you call the animal you're always walking on every time you cross the street?
3. Have you ever heard someone repeating what you just said? This animal does that but with no disrespect at all. What is it?
4. This animal wears a crown, but not exactly on its head. He wears it around his neck. This is one of the reasons he's called the king of the jungle.
5. This animal has 4, but every time he sees you coming home, he suddenly has only 2. He's always happy to see you, no wonder he's called man's best friend.
6. You know having a lion at home is super dangerous. Did you know that you have one of his dear cousins at home? What animal is it?

7. You can't blame this animal for changing too often. He's a master of disguise, and the colors he can change to will leave you amazed, too. What animal am I talking about?

8. This tiny bird has the tiniest wings, and yet he moves them as fast as he can, what is it?

9. In real life, this animal won't become a handsome prince if kissed. But you can be sure that he's the best jumper you'll ever see, what is it?

10. Everybody has touched this bird's wings at least once in their lives, and yet, this bird doesn't use those wings to fly, what is it?

11. If Spiderman got beaten by a spider, then surely Batman got beaten by a...

12. This animal doesn't seem to be special, but if you wait a little longer, a beautiful butterfly will come out of it, what is it?

13. Everybody calls him "Teddy" when he's at home, but this wild animal cannot be at home because he's very dangerous, what is it?

14. This animal doesn't have the largest legs, but it's the tallest animal on Earth. How can that be possible? It must be that very large neck.

15. This animal is also very big, but what you'll notice first is his huge nose. Don't make fun of him because he might hear you with those huge ears.

School Riddles :

1. This thing on the wall is white when it's dirty and black when it's used, what is it?

2. This thing seems hungry all the time; it feeds on everything you use to write, and yet you keep feeding him,
   what is it?
3. This little thing also eats your pencils, but it does that
   little by little until it's satisfied, what is it?
4. Everyone makes mistakes from time to time! Thankfully,
   he's always there to wipe them out clean, what is it?
5. She can show you many things, and you're always surprised at how much she knows. She seems to know it all!
   Who is it?
6. It's the safest place you can store your things, big and
   small. You need a code to open it but not to close it.
7. This person sits where no one can sit, his office is the
   most important, but no one of your classmates wants to
   enter. Who is it?

More fun riddles:

1. You use this thing to play, read, text, and more. It seems
   that people have forgotten that this was created to just
   make calls.
2. Some of them are very fat; some are very flat. Whatever
   their shape, you need a remote if you want to make them
   work. What is it?
3. Many voices come from this little box, but there's no
   inside. Sometimes, you hear music coming from it, but
   there's no band inside. No, you're not crazy. What is it?
4. You won't believe how colorful the sky can be. Thankfully, after the rain has poured, this bow colors the sky.
   What is it?
5. You might need to wear these if it's too bright outside.
   They make everything look dark, but don't be fooled if
   you take them off, you'll see how bright everything is.

3

DIFFICULT RIDDLES

1. You see, your teacher has asked your classmate to answer some questions. You see that your classmate hasn't opened his mouth at all, and yet the teacher says that your classmate has done a very good job. How's that possible?
2. Your dog is on the corner of your block, waiting for you. You rush to meet him, but you can't find him, and yet you're still on the corner of your block. What seems to be the problem?
3. A marathon will take place in your hometown. This marathon will take place between 9 am and noon. You want to participate but are told that only residents can participate. Why aren't you allowed to participate in the race?
4. During the winter, when it's 10 a.m. in the state of California, it's 11 a.m. in the state of Arizona. During the summer, if it's 10 a.m. in California, then it's also 10 a.m. in Arizona. How's that possible?
5. What are the exercises everyone can do when talking?
6. What's the color of the house of the President?

7. What's the country that gets hurt every time you mention it?

8. There are 2 cats in someone's house during the day; at night, there's none. What happened?

9. What lights at night always shine without electricity?

10. I can count to 20 using all of my fingers, and I don't need to start over. How can I do it?

11. There are many pets in Mary's house. His pets include a hamster, a dog, a cat, a rabbit, a mouse, a bird, and a lizard. Mary says that if the dog disappears, all of the animals except for the cat will disappear, too. How's that possible?

12. It takes a person 3 hours to get to Miami from New York City, but it also takes 3 hours to get out of New York City. How's that possible?

13. What do you call a person who is angry because he hasn't eaten yet?

14. This computer doesn't have a keyboard, and yet I can still type on it, what is it?

15. No matter how strong you are, you can't hold it for long, what is it?

16. A cat would be delighted to eat but won't unless he wants to be electrocuted, what is it?

17. If you mix 10 black horses and 10 brown horses, what will you get?

18. What has thousands of letters but is actually written with only 10?

19. What gets dirtier the more you use it to clean yourself?

20. What has the appearance of nothing but fills you up when you're thirsty?

21. We know that at 12:00, the hands of the clock overlap; that is, they touch each other. At what other time do they overlap again?

22. What is the one thing that, if you ever share it, then you never had it?

23. Patrick was one of the most respected and best doctors that have ever existed. He lived 40 years ago and performed many surgeries for many people. All of those surgeries were completely successful. Still, all of his patients are dead. How's that possible?

24. After a robbery, the team is trying to decide to split the plunder among all of the members. Interestingly, they know very well that the bags they stole are mislabeled since this is a common practice to discourage or avoid robberies. The bags are labeled as diamonds, gold and diamonds, and gold.

    How can they know what's inside each bag by opening just one of them?

25. One of your teachers relates how one day, he tried to find a friend at the mall. He said he told his friend that he would be in the food court where all the restaurants are located. He also told him that he would be having lunch at KFC.

    After a while, he realizes that his friend was at the same table where he was eating. How's that possible? How can two people be at the same table and not be able to see each other?

26. Luke is participating in a checkers tournament. He knows how to play very well, and that's why he reaches the final stage of the tournament. Since it's a knockout tournament, every player gets to play only once, unless he wins.

    The first of the tournament, 20 matches were played. There weren't enough players because it was a school day. On the second day, there are more players since it's Saturday and there are no classes. This time, there are

130 players.

How many players are there on the first day? And how many matches were played on the second day?

27. How can you write nine in such a way that if we take one, it becomes ten?

28. When Johny went to the mall with his mom, he found that there were may people. After asking some shoppers, he realized that it was Black Friday, and there were many offers available.

    He asked his mom if she could give him some money to buy a new tablet. Johny saw that the tablet had a 20% discount. Unfortunately, his mom doesn't have enough money at the moment and tells Johny that she will buy it for him next week.

    Johny comes back next week to the mall and sees that the price increased to what it used to be before the Black Friday discounts. By what percentage did the price of the tablet increase?

29. Some days ago, Nick was having dinner with his parents. All of a sudden, there was a power outage. This power outage affected all the city where Nick lives.

    Nick's family still wanted to have dinner, so they lighted 10 candles. Some minutes later, a strong window came through one of the windows and this extinguished five of the candles. Nick and his family don't need to worry anyway since they still have other candles that they can use. At the end of the night, how many candles will they have left?

30. Shawn is on a tour of the jungle. He's always dreamed of visiting this place and now that he's here, he can't wait to enter and see all the animals and plants of the jungle.

    The jungle is divided into two. The western part and the eastern part. It's been divided like that because a large river goes through it. Shawn is the western part of the jungle. There, he has seen many amazing animals he has never seen in his life.

After a couple of hours, he's told that there are even more animals such as giraffes and elephants on the eastern side of the park. Amazed at this, he tells everyone that he wants to go, and so he tells his guide to take him to that side of the park.

After a couple of hours of walking towards the eastern part of the park, they finally find the river. There are only three rivers along the river to cross it. Unfortunately, the other two are very far from where they are, and it would make them even more hours just to get there. So they decide to just use this bridge.

This bridge is very told. The tour guide tells Shawn that the bridge will only be able to resist one person at a time and that the person should not weigh more than 90 kilograms. Shawn weighs 70, but he's carrying a bag that weighs 20 kilograms and another one that weighs just 10 kilograms.

Since the bridge is very old, he cannot cross may time, sho he can't come back to take more things; in other words, he'll have to find a way to carry all his things on one just trip.

How does Shawn manage to cross the bridge?

31. Francis likes to ride his bike. Since he's been a teenager, he's been riding his bike along the border between the United States and Canada. Even though he's a good kid, his family members aren't as well behaved as he is.

    Some of his relatives are smugglers. They ask Francis for help. At first, he refuses to take part in that but feels like he doesn't have any other chance.

    Since that day on, Francis crosses the bridge every weekend on his bike. Interestingly, the police that are on the border don't stop him at any time. It seems weird since he's actually smuggling objects through the border.

What's more interesting is that he doesn't seem to be taking anything across the border. He's only riding his bike back and forth from Canada and the United States.

We know Francis is smuggling something, what is the smuggling?

32. Ryan likes to call his girlfriend when he gets home. Ryan's girlfriend lives on the other side of town, and so they talk on the phone for many hours since they can't see each other.

Ryan's girlfriend's name is Miranda. Miranda has a sister; her name is Roxanne. Unfortunately, Ryan finds a problem every time he calls Miranda. Roxanna and Miranda are twin sister and so they have voices that are very similar. They both also like to prank Ryan.

One of them would always lie to Ryan about who's the one answering the phone while the other would always tell the truth.

How can Ryan tell which one is the one answering the phone?

33. Every country has its own national celebrations. On these occasions, people in these countries go out and enjoy the free time they have with family members and friends.

There's a very national celebration that takes place in Russia every year, and it's called the October Revolution.

In what month do they celebrate it?

34. My friend's mom likes to collect famous paintings. She has collected many through the years, and now her daughter wants to sell some of them. unfortunately, her

mother has told her time and again that she won't seel any painting she has.

After a while, the mother finally agrees to sell some of the paintings she has. Excited, her daughter goes and puts up many signs on the streets and in the newspapers.

She knows very well that many of the paintings have a lot of value. And she also knows that her mother would usually buy 1 painting every time she celebrated her birthday. Since her mother is 80, she thinks that her mother must've collected a lot of paintings.

She's is surprised to find that there are only 20 paintings in her room. She goes to asks her mom, but she tells her that those 20 paintings are the only ones she has bought. How can that be if she's 80 years old and she has bought one painting for every birthday she celebrated?

35. During the physical education class, the teacher asks the students to be in order and to form a line. He calls many students to do some warm-ups and exercises. After a while, he calls one classmate and you to do some tricky warm-ups.

    To do this, he tells you to stand behind your classmate. That's not too difficult; you just have to stand behind your classmate to do it. But for the warm-up to be perfectly executed, your classmate also has to stand behind you.

    How can you and your classmate do that?

36. What's the only 3D object that only has one surface?

37. One father wants to leave a very large inheritance to his sons. His two sons have been very kind to him, and they have worked with him for many years. He now wants to leave something for them.

    He has been thinking about leaving them all his fortune.

His fortunes consist of many rings, jewels, and properties all around the country. The only problem here is that it would be very difficult to place a value to all of these things since there are too many and some of them are very old.

He knows that he might not be able to give them both equal parts of the inheritance. Still, he wants to give both a part of it and so he's planning on dividing his fortune in a way that will leave both of his children happy.

How can the man divide his fortune in such a way that his children will feel happy with it?

38. Alex is a gifted child that's been invited to participate in an international competition in Europe. Many kids from all over the world have also been invited to participate.

    Amazingly, Alex makes it to the finals, and now he has to compete against an Italian kid. The test they have to take might seem to be very simple as the first questions asked about the dates when important events happened.

    Alex and the Italian guy finish their exams, and the judges are amazed at how intelligent these kids are. They try to correct but find you that both Alex and the Italian guy are named Alex; both have the same age, the same writing style, and even the same answers.

    Still, there's a way the judges can find out who's who. How can they do that?

39. You enter a very old shop that sells watches, clocks, and even hourglasses. These hourglasses come in different shapes and forms, but they all h¿work to tell time. Some of them can count up to 15 minutes. Some can count up to an hour.

    The seller tells you that you can count time perfectly with the hourglasses. But there's a problem: some hourglasses can't measure time exactly as you might want to.

For example, if you want to count 13 minutes in an hourglass, then you might have a hard time finding the right hourglass. Most of the hourglasses created here can only count up to 11, 21 or 31. It's hard to find specific hourglasses.

Still, the seller tells you that he can count up to 25 just by using two hourglasses. The hourglasses that the seller wants to use can count up to 21 and 23 minutes.

How can the man count 25 minutes using a 21-minute and a 23-minute hourglass?

40. John, Nathanael, Alex, and Ronald are in a mall trying to find some clothes they can wear to a party. Just as they are going up to the second floor, a huge earthquake occurs and traps everyone inside. The earthquake also causes a power outage so no one can see anything.

    They all need to go out in 12 minutes before the whole building falls down. To get out of the building, they will have to carry a flashlight. But the person who goes out would have to come back into the building to give the flashlight to the others. John is a very athletic guy, so he won't have any problem going out of the building; he can run and be out of the building in just 1 minute.

    Nathanael is a little overweight and will take more time than John. He can get out of the building in 4 minutes. Alex is even much slower then Nathanael. He can exit the building in 5 minutes. Finally, Ronald is also an athletic guy, so he will take just 2 minutes to get out of the building.

    They all need to get out of the building in 12 minutes or less. Someone needs to come back every time to give the flashlight back. Also, even though they all have different abilities and might take longer than others, if they go with a faster person, this one can help them, and so,

they'll have the speed of the one who runs faster.
How will they exit the building?

41. A math teacher is in a very good mood today and so, presents the class with one good riddle. Why is he in such a good mood? The whole class took an exam last week, and he found out that all of his students passed it.

The exam was pretty easy. All they had to do was make some sums and substractions. To do this, they had to study all the numbers they could and not use a calculator. Now that they have been able to do it, they will have to show the teacher that they have truly studied not just to pass the exam, but also to use it in their lives.

The teacher tells them that all numbers use all the vowels: a, e, I, o, and u. But, unfortunately, a person can take a long time trying to find a number that has certain vowels. The teacher says:

"For example, you know that the number "one" contains the vowels o and e. The number "four" contains the letters o and u. The number "eight" contains the vowels e and i. But where's the vowel a? Where can I find it? How much will I have to count until I find a number that has the vowel a?"

Do you know the answer?

42. Francis is a very young man that is visiting this city for the first time. He doesn't know everyone, and no one in this city knows him. After having driven for quite a while in this city, he gets hungry and so he decides to go to a restaurant.

This restaurant makes very good and delicious food. He enters and just wants to order something light because he knows that he will have to continue on his trip. What's special about this restaurant is that there are a lot of elderly people. There are some who are eating with their grandchildren and other family members.

Francis sits at a table and orders what he wants to eat. He's alone but he doesn' feel uncomfortable. An old man approaches the table where Francis is seated and asks him if he can sit there with him. Francis says yes.

As they enjoy their meals, they find out they have a lot of things in common. Both like country music and even the same artists. Both have mothers whose name is Eliane. Both are from the same part of the country, and even both have ordered the same meal. The old man is very touched by all of this and starts to cry a little.

Francis tries to console the man. This man, in turn, tells Francis that he looks a lot like a son he had but who died a while ago in an accident. Francis is very sorry for that and tries to comfort the old man.

The old man tells Francis to tell him that it would make his day if Francis agrees to say, "See you later, daddy," as his lost son used to say. Francis agrees and says, "See you later, daddy." Then, he hugs the old man and sees him leaving the restaurant.

After a while, the waitress comes back with the bill. Francis receives the bill, but he's very surprised to find out something in the bill. What did he find out?

43. At Sophie's house, there are some books that are her mom gave her as a gift. Her mom knows very well that she likes to read and so she has given her a lot of books. Every time her classmates come to visit her or to play with her, they can see that there are a lot of books.

Her father has also given her some books. He hasn't given Sophie as much as her mother, but he still finds the way to buy the books he knows she's going to love.

One day, while they're at school, Sophie's friend asks her how many books her father has given her. Sophie tells her that her father has not given her as many books as her mother has. Still, Sophie's friend wants to know the exact number.

Sophie tells her:

"The books that my father has given me are these: All except three are history books. All except three are fiction books. All except three books are novels. And all except three are math books."

Can you tell how many books Sophie has?

44. A math teacher is very happy with his students since he knows that they are very intelligent and have been able to answer any questions. After having taught them for a great part of the year, he decides to retire. As a surprise, the principal will come and visit the class for a final assessment of the students. He wants to know if the students have really learned a lot of math or not.

The teacher is very confident and trusts that his students will give the principal a very good impression. Still, he knows that these last weeks he has been teaching some very difficult lessons. Knowing this, he devises a plan so that everyone will seem to know the answers to all of the questions the principal will throw them

Finally, the day comes. The principal arrives and then proceeds to enter the classroom. All the students greet him, and the principal asks for a math book. After picking one book, he starts asking the first question. Surprised that everybody raises their hand, he tells the teacher to pick one up at random to answer the question. The teacher does that and one of the students is chosen to answer. To the principal's surprise, the student was able to answer correctly.

The principal continues with the next question, and the same thing happens again. The student is able to answer the question correctly but everybody raises their hands. This makes the principal think that everybody knows the answer.

This occurs a couple of times more until he finally realizes that everybody knows the answer. Satisfied, he congratulates the teacher and tells the students that they have done a very good job. After this, the principal goes back to his office to continue working.

The teacher then turns to the students and tells them that they have also done a very good job by cooperating with him on the plan.

What was the teacher's plan to fool the principal?

45. Albert and Alexander are very good friends. They have known each other for quite a while, and they have visited each other's houses many times. That's why it comes as no surprise when Alexander visits Albert and Albert's mother tells him to wait inside the house.

Alexander sits in the living room and decided to watch some TV. Before being able to turn the TV, Albert's mother tells him that Albert left his laptop on for him if he wants to play with it. alexander loves playing videogames on Albert's laptop, so he stands up and goes to where the laptop is.

The laptop is already on, so he doesn't have to turn it to himself. The only problem is that he needs the password. Albert's mother knows the password but she tells Alexander that Albert has left the password written on a piece of paper under the laptop. Albert knows that Alexander has a quick mind and that he will be able to decipher the right password.

Under the laptop, Alexander finds the password. Well, it's not really a password. What he actually finds is a list of numbers and words. They don't seem to have any connection. They're just written in an order that makes Alexander doubt, and he starts thinking if he will ever find the password.

The paper contained this for Alexander:

"I know that you will enjoy trying to guess the right password for my laptop. You don't have to worry very much about the password since it's here in front of your own eyes. Just follow the clues:

1 here 2 love 3 Rome 1 water 2 today 1 reason 3 like"

Can you decipher the password?

46. There are some codes that secret agent Julian has to decipher in order to find what the evil doctor Frank wants to do. He already knows the plan. What he needs to find out is when he's going to do it.

Secret agent Julian has enlisted the help of his best friend, Nick, in order to decipher the riddle. Doctor Frank wants to unleash a dangerous chemical into the atmosphere. To do this, he will have to find the best time of the year when the weather is perfect.

Secret agent Julian finds some papers that he thinks are the clues he needs to find when doctor Frank is going to release the dangerous chemical. The paper reads like this:

"The first month is 1017

The second month is 628

The fifth month is 1353

We'll release the bomb in 1999."

Secret agent Julian thinks he has found the right answer. Are you also available to decipher when the doctor is going to release the dangerous chemical?

47. Some prankster has been doing some bad things to many people all around the city. The police have set out to catch them, but they haven't been able to get them so far.

One day, the police discover that they're going to appear in the city fair near where the airport is. They are planning on pranking the guests and even the city's mayor. Knowing their plan, the police lay out a plan to finally catch them.

At 2 p.m., the pranksters arrive, and they try to prank the mayor. Knowing that this would occur, a group of policemen arrived as fast as they could and captured the pranksters. Thinking that they can escape, they run as fast as they can.

Thankfully, all the pranksters are caught, and everyone in town celebrates. They congratulate the police and they start to think about what they're going to do with them. Later that day, the police relate how they were able to capture the pranksters.

They say that they already knew very well what they would do, but they had some problems with their headlight and flashlights. The police said that even though it was impossible to make them work, they were still able to capture them.

How was the police able to capture the pranksters if their headlights weren't working and the flashlight wasn't working either?

48. Ariana is visiting a city very far from where she lives. She's there to visit a friend. She has tried to get to her friend's city as far as she can, but her friend lives so far that she had to make a stop at a motel in the middle of nowhere.

    She first parks the car she's been driving and then she enters the motel. The motel's receptionist tells her that she needs to pay $25 if she wants to have a room. She accepts and pays, and then, she's given the keys to her room.

She walks up to the fourth floor and sees that there a lot of rooms on that floor. She sees her room and then enters. While she gets ready to take a shower, she hears a knock on the door. At first, she asks who it is, but nobody answers.

Some minutes later, the same thing happens, but this time she opens the door and finds a large man with a hat standing there. She is very surprised, and it seems that the man is also very surprised. The man tells her:

"I'm so sorry if I scared you. I thought this was my room. I apologize."

The woman accepts the man's apology but still finds it very suspicious, and so she calls the receptionist to alert her of the man. It seems that the man was very honest and, he may have possibly gotten confused. Why didn't Ariana believe the man's apology?

49. Joan's mother was at a fair with her daughter and her dogs. She wanted to bring a prize home and, to be fair with her, she's been very close many times today.

    She wanted to play darts, and she did it pretty well. She threw all the darts, but still, she lost to another person. She then wanted to play basketball but there were a lot of people and so she couldn't play. Her daughter has also been playing but she doesn't really want to try to get a prize.

    Her dogs have been in the dog section, and they have been having the best days of their lives so far. Finally, all the family decides it's time to live. Before leaving, though, Joan's mother wants to try one more game. Everyone thinks that's not a good idea and tells her that she shouldn't play again.

    After insisting, they let Sophie's mother play one last time. This time, she goes to a clown, and this clown tells her that she can win any prize she wants if she's able to decipher a simple riddle. They think it's a very good idea and so they allow her to play. The riddle is very simple: Sophie's mother just has to tell the clown how many R's are there in the following sentence.

"Ryan, Robert, and Ronald Reasoned that they had enough money to buy everything they needed for the school party and more."

Sophie's mother started to think deeply for a minute and then said:

"It's easy; there are only 3 R."

The clown laughed a little at her and told her that it wasn't true. Sophie's mother was very sad and started to go to the car. At that, Sophie told her mom that she knew the right answer:

"What's the answer, little girl?" said the clown.

"There are 9 Rs"

When the clown heard the answer, he told everyone that he had finally found someone who was able to decipher the riddle. The clown gave Sophie the chance to choose whatever prize she wanted.

The whole family went back home with a huge teddy bear. Even Sophie's mother was very happy that her daughter found the answer.

How was Sophie able to tell the right answer?

50. On a rainy day, John and his grandchildren are in the middle of a conversation. They have decided to stay in since it's raining every much outside. The kids are a little sad since they wanted to go outside to play with his grandfather.

Noticing this, John decides to tell them stories about the time when he was very young and the things he used to do to have fun. Some of the kids are very surprised because they had never heard of what their Grandpa is telling them. John relates how he didn't have a phone, and nobody knew about the internet.

The kids are amazed and are really left wondering how Grandpa could have any fun if he didn't have any of the things they do now. It's not all bad, though. John tells his grandkids that when he was a child, he was able to go to the movies with his parents and even with some of his friends. There weren't as many special effects as there are now, but he still enjoyed it.

He also relates the time when his parents bought a new TV. The kids imagine that he's talking about a flat-screen, HD TV, and start asking where it is. John laughs a little and tells them that, back in those days, they didn't have a flat-screen TV. The TV back then was very big and was called "black-and-white TV."

At that, one of John's grandkids jumps out of his seat and stops his grandfather. He says that what John is saying is a lie. John accepts that he was actually telling a lie, but it was because he wanted to prank them.

How did one of John's grandkids find out that his grandfather was lying?

51. The social studies teacher is relating many stories to his students. She's been a person who has traveled all around the world and so knows a lot of things and also a lot of people. As she continues to tell them about one of her trips, one of the students asks her about the most bizarre experience she ever had.

    The teacher stops to think deeply for a while, trying to remember. It's pretty difficult for her since she has traveled a lot. Nodding her head, she thinks she has found the right experience to tell.

    She stands in front of all of the class and starts telling

them the story:

"Many years ago, when I was visiting South Africa, I stayed at one of my friend's house. She had been living in South Africa for many years, so she knew where the best places to hang out where.

After some weeks, we went to visit one of her relatives that were also living in South Africa. When we get there, we find that there was a problem. My friend's family was discussing marriage. They didn't know what to do with a widow, her husband.

It was chaotic, to say the least. We didn't know what to say or do, and my friend felt a little embarrassed. She apologized and then we went back home as fast as we could. On the way home, she started telling me that one man wanted to marry his widow's cousin. When I heard that, I was surprised and I couldn't believe it, but at the same time, I understood that my friend was kidding and that she didn't want to tell me the truth."

The class was a little surprised, too. They've never heard a story like that. But, ow as the teacher, sure that her friend was lying to her?

52. Taylor and her friends are at a party. The party was taking place at Harry's house. Many of her friends' parents also came to the party. They were all talking, eating, or dancing. They were having a lot of fun.

One of Taylor's friends' name is Jane. Jane has also another sister. Jane's sister's name is Emma. Taylor's father notes that Jane and Emma look very similar and so asks them if they are twins.

The girls, intelligent as they are, reply that they are not twins, even though it's very obvious that they are twins. Taylor's father can't believe this, and so asks their mother.

To his astonishment, their mother says that they are not twins but that they do look identical.

How can this possible of they are not twins?

53. On a faraway land, people are punished with death if they are found stealing from the queen. It's not really common to find people who dare do that, and so it's very rare to hear of people who are punished to die. Of course, from time to time, there are some people who think they can fool the queen and her guards. For example, there were two me who, on the day, entered the queen's palace that was close to a river. One of the men disguised himself as a guard, and the other men waited swam in the river so that he could climb the walls of the palace. Realizing that the walls were too tall to climb, the man who planned to disguise himself as a guard told him that he could try to open the door to let him in. as you can see, this theft was not well planned. Still, they wanted to try it and see what happened. Incredibly, they were able to make inside the palace. Now they had to find the queen's safe. They knew that the safe was on the fifth floor. The funny thing is that they couldn't use an elevator since there weren't any. They had to walk up the stairs. You can already imagine how tired they must've been when they reached the fifth floor. Tired as they were, they didn't want to give up on their mission. They started searching for the safe but couldn't find it. One of them even wanted to throw the towel when, finally, they found the safe. They got out of the building as fast as they could. They didn't walk but actually run down the stairs. Unfortunately for the robbers, there were some guards waiting for them on the first floor. One of the men was captured while the other jumped out of the window and into the river. The guards were surprised and thought that the man couldn't have

survived, but when they went to see outside the window, they saw that the man was still alive and was swimming to the other side of the river. The guards kept looking for the missing thieve but couldn't find him. since they couldn't find the man, they tried the man they could capture. They brought the man in front of the queen and her advisers. The man knew very well what could happen to him. The queen didn't want to carry out the penalty, and so told the man that he would be given another form of execution if he told who the other man is and where he is. At first, he decides not to tell the queen but then realized that he wants to keep living and so tell the queen everything he knows about the man. The queen is satisfied with the man's answers and tells him that he will not be executed on the spot but that he will be punished anyway. The queen asks her advisers about another form of execution. Her advisers give her a very good alternative, and the queen agrees with them. In the end, the man seems to be released free out of the castle, and he goes to his house with his family. He's also told never to return to the castle. What method of execution did the adviser recommend to the queen?

4

FIENDISH RIDDLES

1. If John has 4 brothers and all of them have one sister, how many children do John's parents have?
2. What kind of people will you only find in Russia?
3. If it's happy, it waves, if it's sad, it won't move. If it sees you, it waves; if you're gone, it doesn't move. What is it?
4. Who has many pets in his house but doesn't own one of them?
5. There are 5 cats in Dave's house. His mom doesn't want to have many cats, so she has decided to give some away. Dave is obviously very sad, but he thinks he can have more cats again in the future. How can he do this without bringing more cats into the house?
6. How can you change the TV channel if the control remote doesn't have enough numbers?
7. Lisa's house only has 5 rooms. Her house has one bathroom, one kitchen, one living room, and one dining room. There's only one bedroom, and yet there are more than 5 beds. How's that possible?
8. Lisa has been receiving some new toys lately. She feels she has many toys and so she wants to share her toys with her brother. Her brother less her that if she decides

to give those toys to him, she'll never have them back. Why does he say so?

9. Mary has been traveling to the UK, Canada, Australia, and New Zealand. She only speaks one language, and yet she can easily communicate with everyone who lives in those countries. How's that possible?

10. The language that comes from France is called French; the language that comes from Germany is called German; the language that comes from China is called Chinese, so the language that comes from Canada is called...

11. You haven't told anyone that you're in fourth grade, but your classmates have found about it. How's that possible?

12. There's always someone who's following you, and yet you can touch him, and you can't talk to him. What is it?

13. It seems that everything that has four legs can walk easily: a dog, a tiger, a lizard. But what has 4 legs but can't walk at all?

14. You don't need to push it or even touch it to break it. What is it?

15. If people keep their money in banks, where do polar bears get to keep their money?

16. David's grandson is seven years old. The weird thing is that the sum of his age digits is exactly the same as his grandson's. How's that possible?

17. I'm in a very dark room, but I'm still able to read. How can I do that?

18. It powers your computer, your TV, your phone, your refrigerator and many other things you need. It would be safe to say that it is electricity, but that's not the right answer. What is it?

19. Many years ago, people didn't have phones to talk to each other. They didn't have the internet to search for

stuff. They didn't have a TV to watch their favorite TV series. But we use something they discovered to make them work. What is it?

20. What has been framed but is not in prison?
21. What's between an "I" and another "I"?
22. What is always "too tired" to work?
23. There was a man, son of a prince, who wanted to travel abroad to a very faraway land. His dad found out about this and decided to help his son with some money. The prince, along with his son, started planning all that he needed to do to be safe in the new country, and he even gave his son some tips on where to stay or eat.

    The prince realized that his child would need a little more money. He only needed one thousand dollars more. He came up with a very good plan. He went to the bank immediately, and he looked for the manager of that bank. When he finally found the bank manager, he told him:

    "My son is going to travel to a very distant land, and he needs a little more money. I was wondering if this is a good place I could take a loan from."

    The bank manager, realizing that he was a rich man, gladly accepted the petition of the prince. He answered the prince:

    "Sure, sir, this is the best place you can ever find. How much does your son need?"

    "He needs $1000"

    "You will have to leave something to give you the loan."

    "No problem. I can leave my crown here.

    The bank manager didn't know what to say. He had never seen a crown, and this was the first time he had one in his hands. The strange thing about all of this is that the crown exceeded by a lot the loan. The bank manager thought that the prince was a fool for leaving such precious crown filled with so many jewels and gold here in the bank.

After taking the money, the prince gave it to his son, and then, the son parted. After a while, the son came back and he was even able to bring some money, enough to pay the loan. Without any delay, the prince and his son went to the bank to pay the loan.

When the bank manager saw them entering, he laughed at them, and then he accepted the payment. Curious, the bank manager asked the prince why he had left his crown when he could've left something of lesser value.

The prince started telling the bank manager:

"Before my son left the city, I was advised to keep all my jewels and my money safe because there were some robbers who were looking for my fortune. I didn't know where to store all of it. At first, I was able to store some of my jewels in some of my friends' houses."

"What does that have to do with your crown, sir?", asked the bank manager

So now, the question is, why did the prince leave his crown at the bank?

24. Katy was thinking about going to her friend's house to ask for help with some homework the teacher had left for the class. The only problem was that she didn't know exactly where her friend Karissa lived.

    After asking a couple of people where Karissa lives, she set out to go with her parents at 5 p.m. after having lunch. Before leaving, she first had to make sure that Jarissa was going to be home. Most of the time, Karissa goes to her piano classes after classes and so Katy is worried she might not find her at home.

    Thankfully, she somehow managed to communicate with Karissa. It's weird because she didn't have to speak to her at all to agree on a time to meet.

How's that possible?

25. On a rainy day, Martin and his friends are going to the mall to buy some new videogames they can play at his house. Before going to the mall, they make sure they have enough money to buy all the games they want. They decide to just bring $100 dollars.

It's a special day for the mall, and so there are a lot of discounts in many stores. One of those stores is the videogame store. They have a lot of discounts available to everyone and that's what makes the guys go to the mall today even though it's a rainy day.

When they finally get to the mall, they try to fins the videogame store. After finding the store, they find out that the store has lowered the prices of many popular games. Now, the soccer game costs only $40, while the hockey game costs only $20.

As mentioned, the guys have $100 dollars, so they have more than enough to buy both games. They line up to buy the games and they see that the person who is in front of them gives the seller 40 dollars, and he's given the hockey game without hesitation. The seller didn't even ask for which game he wanted to choose. He just gave it to the customer.

When it's finally their turn, they give the seller 40 dollars, too, but the seller starts asking them what game they wanted to take. It's weird since they weren't expecting to be asked.

Why did the seller ask the guys which game they wanted to take?

26. A woman named Muriel Norah is married to a very nice man. This man wanted to have children with Muriel, and so they all now have 7 children. Six of them are already in

the house working and helping her mom while the other one is still in her mom's belly.

- ○ The names of the children are as follows:

- ○ Dominic, he likes to play the piano.

- ○ Rebecca, she likes to play the guitar

- ○ Miranda; she loves to sing with her other siblings

- ○ Farrah; she likes to play the violin

- ○ Solange; she's the youngest. She has started to learn how to play the drums.

- ○ Laura; also likes music a lot but she doesn't know how to play an instrument yet.

- ○ Now that you name the names of the children of Muriel and her husband, can you guess the name of the next child?
  1. Simon

  2. Raul

  3. Linda

27. Danny's science teacher is asking his class some difficult science questions. Most of the time, when the teacher asks this type of question, it's because he wants to give his students a chance to earn more points and have higher grades. Danny has been studied hard all this week, and so he knows how to answer many of the questions the teacher is throwing at him and his classmates. Actually, he has been answering most of them. The teacher notices this and

he asks Danny one difficult question to make him think:
How can I get milk and water in one glass?" Danny, confi-
dently, answers the question: "That's easy. You just have to
pour milk into the glass, and then you can add water." The
teacher knows that Danny would answer that way. After
all, the question doesn't seem to have a very difficult answer. But, the teacher adds: "But, what I don't want the water and the milk in the glass to mix with each other?" Danny
says: "That's impossible. They will always have to mix together if they're in a glass." The teacher tells Danny and the
whole class that it isn't impossible. There's a way to put water and milk in the same glass without both mixing. How's
that possible?

28. Some days ago, Maria entered her house and found out
that there were some broken glasses inside. It seemed that
someone had broken into her house but later found out
that nothing was robbed. It seemed weird because the door
wasn't forced and so it didn't seem to have been a robbery. Still, she was still a little worried about it and wanted
to know who did it. She began suspecting that some of her
neighbors may have done it. Since only 4 of her neighbors
knew how to enter her house without a key, she went to aks
all of them. Their names were Lauren Smith, Raphael Smith,
Mark Smith, and Joanne Smith. As you may have noticed,
all of them are related but live in different houses. After
Maria asked them, she still couldn't come up with the right
person. Why? Because everyone kept denying it. In the end,
she received a message from a friend. The paper was a note
where it detailed who did it. interestingly, there was only
one sentence: "? Smith. He was the one who did it" At that
moment, Maria understood who had done it. Do you know
who did it?

29. There were two friends who were playing in a maze. After playing for many hours, they thought to have found the answer. Unfortunately for them, that was just the second part of the maze. After entering into the second part of the maze, they knew that they would eventually find the exit. Finally, they found the exit. But, interestingly, there were two doors in front of them. Both were exits, and they could choose any of them to get out of the maze. The first door had a large room of freezing snow behind it. It was so cold that no one could've been able to bear it for more than 5 minutes without freezing to death. The second door had a large room where there was a lot of heat and sand. All this heat was powered by the summer sun that was above the guys. It was so unbearably hot that no one could've been able to stand it for more than 5 minutes. It was a tough choice, and both friends were arguing for a while, which one to choose. They didn't know which one to choose until they found out a way to get out of the maze through one of those doors without suffering any injury. Which door did they choose, and what did they do?

30. A person wanted to build a wall in the middle of his town to protect part of his property. After consulting many people and experts at construction, he deiced to call his best friends to ask them, too. What this man wanted was to fence off the greatest amount of land using as few materials as possible. His first friend, whose name is Bruno, was a doctor, and he knew a lot about how people would feel if they were outside the wall. Hence, he constructed a wall that encircled all the property with many doors. He said that having s many doors a possible would decrease the number of materials used. That was true, but the man didn't like it, saying that he didn't want people being able to enter his property at any moment. His second friend, whose

name is Ruben, had another plan for the wall. He wanted to divide his whole property into two. He wanted to build a wall in the middle of his property. This would undoubtedly decrease the number of materials for the wall, but that would be because of not using them. That's why the man he didn't like Ruben's plan. His third friend, whose name is Veronica, had another plan. She was a very intelligent woman, and she tried to tell the man that he wouldn't have to bring so many materials to build a wall if he followed her plan. When the man saw what Veronica did, he was so impressed that he decided to follow her plan. What was Veronica's plan?

5

CHRISTMAS RIDDLES!

1. Like the stars that hang above in the sky, you hang us around your house and your Christmas tree. What are we?
2. When you're filled with food, you don't want to eat anymore. When I'm stuffed, everyone wants to eat me. What am I?
3. What kind of cane does Santa use?
4. What's a pineapple?
5. Who's always eating snowcones?
6. I'm all over the house giving a ring, trying to get someone to notice me. What am I?
7. His head is full of snowflakes. He must be a...

6

ANSWERS FOR FUN RIDDLES

Animals Riddles:

1. A Panda bear
2. A zebra. The white lines you see on the street are called zebra crossing.
3. A parrot
4. The lion
5. The dog
6. The cat. He's a feline. That means that he's related to the lion; they are part of the same "family."
7. The chameleon
8. The hummingbird
9. The frog
10. The chicken
11. A bat
12. The caterpillar
13. The bear
14. The giraffe
15. The elephant

About school

1. The blackboard
2. The pencil case
3. The sharpener
4. The eraser
5. The teacher
6. The locker
7. The principal

More Fun Riddles:

1. The cell phone
2. The TV
3. The radio
4. The rainbow
5. Sunglasses

7

ANSWERS FOR DIFFICULT RIDDLES:

1. Your classmate was taking a written exam.
2. A block has 4 corners; you're on the wrong corner
3. You don't in your hometown anymore.
4. During the winter, some states "change" the time. This is called Daylight Saving Time. Depending on the time of year, clocks can fall back one hour or move forward one hour. Of course, not all states obey this rule; one of those states is Arizona. So, during certain months of the year, Arizona and California can or cannot follow the same schedule.
5. Jumping to conclusions and beating around the bush.
6. The President lives in the White House
7. S-Pain
8. Cats are nocturnal animals. That means that, during the night, they tend to get out of the house.
9. The stars
10. I'm also using my toes to count.
11. The cat can eat all the other animals.

12. If you're trying to get out of New York City, driving will take you more than 3 hours. But on a plane, you can be in Miami in a little more than 3 hours.
13. "Hangry"
14. It's a tablet
15. Breathe
16. A computer's mouse
17. A stable
18. Post Office
19. Soap
20. Water
21. 1:05
22. A secret
23. He was a very famous doctor 40 years ago. It doesn't matter if all the surgeries he performed were successful, all his patients must've died.
24. First, you have to open the bag that says, "gold and diamonds." You'll find that there aren't gold and diamonds together in that bag. You will likely find that there's only gold or diamonds. Having that in mind, now you can open the other bags knowing what's inside them because all of them are mislabeled.
25. They're actually at the same table, but they're not looking at each other. They are turning their backs on each other.
26. the number of players is always how many matches there are plus 1. The number of matches is always the number of players minus one. So, there were 21 players on the first day, and there were 149 matches on the second day. All of this is possible since it's a knockout tournament.
27. To know the answer to this, you have to think of the Roman equivalent of the number nine, which is IX. If you

take the "I," you'll have the X left. The X is the Roman numeral for the number ten

28. The answer is 25%. Confused? If you take 20% of something, the object has a new value. You would need a 25% increase in the new value to equal what the object used to cost.

29. What's left are the five that weren't extinguished

30. To cross the bridge, he would have to juggle both bags as he's walking the bridge.

31. He's smuggling his clothes

32. Does Miranda lie? Imagine that Roxanne is the one who always tells the truth, and Mirana is the one who always lies. If Roxanne picks up the phone, she will say yes. If Miranda picks up, she will say no. It's pretty obvious, then, that I must've been talking to Roxanne. Now, if we assume that Miranda is telling us the truth and not Roxanne: If Roxanne picks up the phone, she will say yes. If Miranda picks up the phone, she will say no. It's obvious, then, that I must've been talking to Roxanne.

33. This is a tricky one. The October revolution actually happened in November. To understand this, you need to know that we didn't use to count time as we do now. The way the months are ordered today is called a calendar. Today's calendar is called the Gregorian calendar. Before the Gregorian calendar, there used to be another calendar that was a little similar but had a lot of mistakes; that calendar was called the Julian calendar. One of the mistakes the Julian calendar had is that it was many days behind the right date. When we finally made the change to the Gregorian calendar, we corrected many dates, and of those is the celebration of the October Revolution. It's called October Revolution because it took place in Octo-

ber in the Julian calendar but it's actually celebrated In November because that's the right date.

34. Her right date of birth is November 29. That means that she only has collected a picture once every four years.

35. You and your classmate would have to turn your back on each other.

36. A sphere

37. To make it fair for both, one child can divide the inheritance, and the other can be the first to claim the part he wants the most.

38. It's easy to identify who comes from America and who doesn't just by seeing the way he writes dates. Americans tend to write dates like this: month/day/year. That's not the case in most parts of the world where the preferred order is day/month/year.

39. You have to take both hourglasses and tip them over. The 21-minute hourglass will end in just 21 minutes. When that one is finished, flip it over again. When the 23-minute hourglass is over, the 21-minute hourglass will have measured 2 minutes more. Flip the 21-minute hourglass again, and you'll see the remaining two minutes being counted two. 23 minutes + 2 minutes is 25 minutes.

40. First, you have to remember that someone needs to come back to return the flashlight.
    1. John and Ronald will get out of the building. Since John is faster than Rinakd, he will help him get out of the building faster. It will take just 2 minutes.
    2. John will come back and give someone else the flashlight. It will take him just one minute.
    3. Alex will get out with Nathanael. This will take them just 5 minutes.
    4. Ronald will return in just two minutes.

5. John and Ronald will get out of the building. This will take them just 2 minutes.

6. 2 minutes+ 1 minute+ 5 minutes + 2 minutes + 2 other minutes equals 12 minutes.

41. One thousand is the first number that uses the letter "a."

42. The old man had told the waitress that his son would pay for his meal.

43. She has just 4 books. One history book, one math book, one fiction book, and one novel.

44. The plan of the teacher was very simple. Everyone would have to raise their hands; that way, the principal would believe that all the students knew the answer. The point was that those who really knew the answer would raise their right hands, and those who didn't would raise their left hands. The teacher would pick up one from those who raised their right hands.

45. HOMEWORK The number corresponds to the letter of the words that's next to it.

46. It would be September. Having in mind the month of January as seen in the example, 10 corresponds to the letter J in the alphabet. 1 corresponds to the fact that January is the first month of the year. 7 is the number of letters the month of January has.

47. It was daylight; that's why they were able to capture them without any problems.

48. The woman has reason to be suspicious because if it had really been where the man was stating, he wouldn't have knocked on the door.

49. "Ryan, Robert, and Ronald Reasoned that they had enough money to buy everything they needed for the school party and more." That's 9 Rs.

50. He realized his Grandpa was lying because people back then didn't call it "black-and-white TV." They just called it TV

51. A widow's husband is already dead; that's why she's a widow. Therefore, he can't marry anyone.

52. They are actually triplets, not twins. That means that they are three identical sisters rather than just 2.

53. The advisers told the king to let the man die of old age.

8

ANSWERS FOR FIENDISH RIDDLES

1. 6 children. John and his 4 brothers have the same sister. So, they are 6 in total.
2. You will find Russians in Russia
3. A dog's tail
4. The vet
5. He only needs to keep 2 cats. In just a couple of months, they will multiply.
6. You can stand up and press the buttons on the TV
7. All of them are in one bedroom
8. All of the gifts were given by her brothers. If she gives the toys to her brother, she will be giving them back.
9. The same language is spoken in the UK, Canada, Australia, and New Zealand.
10. English is spoken in Canada
11. You don't need to tell your classmates. They already know! After all, they're in the same grade as you are.
12. Your shadow
13. A table
14. A promise

15. Snowbanks

16. 5+0 equals 5.

17. The person is reading Braille

18. The charger

19. Electricity

20. A picture

21. A nose

22. A bicycle

23. Because he needed a place to store his crown. remember that he told the manager that someone was trying to steal it and that he couldn't find a place where to store it. The prince used the bank as a place where to store his crown.

24. They were texting. That's why they didn't need to speak a word.

25. To understand this, you need to remember that $40 would get you a hockey game while $20, a soccer game. It's obvious that the person in front of the guys in line paid with two $20 bills. The seller didn't have a problem knowing that the person was looking for the hockey game. If he hadn't wanted the hockey game, he would've paid with just one $20 bill.
The guys paid with a $40 bill, and they were many, so the seller had to ask if they wanted just one hockey game or two soccer games.

26. A. Simon.
Why?
Because the first letters of all the names of the people mentioned in this story correspond to the names of the musical notes.

27. To do that, Danny would have to first put water or milk into the glass and then freeze it. Then, after it's frozen,

put the other into the glass. That way, they're not being mixed.

28. It was Mark Smith.

    This was possible to decipher since the paper read "QUESTION MARK Smith." So, Maria questioned Mark because he had done it.

29. They chose the second door. They did that since they knew that the sun was powering the heat in the room behind the second door. When night fell, they would just walk through it.

30. Her plan was to just encircle the man's house and leave everything outside. That way, his house would be surrounded by a wall, and he wouldn't have wasted a lot of materials.

9

ANSWERS FOR CHRISTMAS RIDDLES

1. Christmas lights
2. A turkey
3. A candy cane
4. The child of a Christmas tree and an apple
5. Snowman
6. Bells
7. Snowman

2

RIDDLES FOR KIDS
AGES 9-12

10

FUN RIDDLES

1. This animal has the tail of a beaver but looks a lot like a duck when you see him from the front. It's ok if you haven't heard of him, he lives the secret life of a pet in Australia, what is it?
2. What has four wheels but can never be faster than a car?
3. How do you get police help very quickly?
4. How do you make white clothes turn black?
5. If you want to see the world in a better way, you would have to see it through these. What are they?
6. What happens at the end of every movie?
7. What kind of powers do superheroes have?
8. What kind of people invented the Smart TV and the smartphone?
9. What is the stone that has a lot of animals living in it?
10. What's the alarm that needs to eat to work?
11. Which hand is the most useful if you want to write something?
12. What do a basketball game and a cave have in common?
13. What do the ocean and your friends have in common?
14. Why do snowmen like eating vegetables?

15. Why does the golfer have to change his clothes all the
    time?
16. Why is it so hard for the skeleton to do exercise?

11

DIFFICULT RIDDLES

1. There are 20 people in one classroom. You start counting everyone but realizes that there are only 19. You count again but keep getting the same result. What seems to be the problem?
2. You need a male dog and a female dog to have puppies. Most of the time, dogs have 7 puppies. After taking care of your male and female dog, you see that, after 9 months, there are now 14 puppies. How's that possible?
3. If you hop on a bus, you'll see that there are a certain number of seats to the right and to the left. On this bus, you'll see 100 seats, but you've been told there are 101 seats. Where's the missing seat?
4. In a very crowded part of New York City, many people who have come from very parts of the world get together to talk to the mayor. Some of them are from Germany, Italy, and Canada, but most of them come from France. All of them need to agree on speaking one language so that the mayor can understand them. In what language will they speak to the mayor?
5. Have you ever been to a library? If so, then you know very well that there are thousands and thousands of

books and a librarian who takes care of them. In this library, the great majority of people who come to read here are students of a nearby school. There are a lot of students, and they always have to wear their uniforms if they want to enter the library; if not, the librarian can take them out of the library. Two students want to enter but one of them has forgotten his uniform, so he asks his classmate:

"If you lend me your uniform, I'll be able to enter and get the book that I want to read. It will only take me 15 minutes."

"Ok, but only for 15 minutes."

After 25 minutes, the student comes out of the library with the book in his hand. The other classmate asks him:

"You said that you would only read for 15 minutes. Why did you stay to read longer?"

To which he replies:

"I was reading for 15 minutes. It didn't take me more than 15 minutes."

The student is right. It actually took him 15 minutes. He didn't break his promise. So, what seems to be the problem?

6. A rock band is made up of many people who know how to play musical instruments. They rehearse every day to play very well. Still, you see that they don't seem to be very intelligent people. After all, there's a poster on their room that says:

"C,D,E,F,G,A,B"

It's pretty obvious that these people don't even know the alphabet. Or, are you wrong? What's wrong with the poster?

7. What has many keys but can't open a door?

8. There are many types of keys that open any type of doors. What's the only type of key that can open bananas?

9. Five years ago, you were five years younger. In 5 years, you will be 5 years older than now. What will you be in 10 years?

10. Some months of the year have more than 30 days; others have less than 31. What's the month that has 28 days?

11. In the ocean, you'll find many animals: turtles, fish, and whales. What's the only animal that's king on land but not in the sea?

12. You are hearing a conversation between three people. Even though you're close enough to hear everything they're saying, you can only hear two voices. What must the other person be doing?

13. I must have a very good taste because everyone stops and stares every time I change my colors. What am I?

14. The more you use me to dry, the wetter I get. What am I?

15. Every summer, Dave and Jane, a couple from Norway, go on a trip to a very luxurious hotel in Iceland that is close to the beach

During their stay, Dave lost his wallet when he was in the pool. After carefully searching for the wallet, Jane puts up a sign that says that the wallet is lost and that a reward will be given to whoever finds it. Jane gives some details about the wallet: it's brown, large, and has a small Norwegian flag inside. The problem is, everyone seems to have their countries' own flag inside their wallets and no one really knows how the Norwegian flag looks like.

Some hours after putting up the sign, a man tells Jane that he's found the wallet. When asked how he found the wallet, he replied:

"I just had to look at the flag of Iceland to find your husband's wallet."

How did the man find Dave's wallet?

16. If a husband and a wife want to leave their inheritance to their children, what do they need to do first?

17. At a clinic, a couple is told by their doctor that they can find out if their kids have any inherited illness with the help of a new device he has invented. Surprised, but incredulous, the couple decides to try it out.

They bring their 3 children into the doctor's room. As the doctor prepares the device, he tells them that the device will emit a high-pitched sound every time a child is healthy.

First, the doctor uses it to see if the first child has any problem. Everyone can hear the sound the device produces, so everyone knows he's healthy. Then, the second child is examined. He's also found healthy. Finally, the doctor continues to use his device to find if there's any problem with the last child.

As the doctor examines the last child, the device doesn't produce any sound. It's very weird. The doctor tries to use it again, but the device doesn't produce any sound at all.

Worried, the parents of the child ask the doctor if there's any problem with the child. The doctor tells them that they don't have to worry about the child because the problem is them.

What seems to be the problem?

18. Some people are trying to get into a private party. In order to get into this party, people have to answer with the right number.

One person comes up to the guard. The guard says: "12". The person, thinking deeply for a minute, thinks he has the right answer and so answers "6." The guard nods and lets him in.

Another person also comes up to the guard. This time, the guard says: "6." After thinking for a minute, this person answers, "3."

From behind, another person has also been trying to get into the party. After seeing how the other two men answered, he thinks he's got the right answer. After he comes up to the guard, the guard says, "10." Confident, he says, "5."

"I'm sorry, but I can't let you in," says the guard.

At this, another man comes up and answers correctly.

What was the right answer?

19. At one school, there are one hundred students. Before the last day of school begins, the principal tells the students that they can go home early if they pass a simple test.

The principal tells them each one of them needs to hand their teacher their history books. But the principal tells them that any student will be picked at random, and he will have to say, "everyone before me has brought his history book." If he's right, he will let all the students go home early; if not, the students will have to stay 2 hours more after classes finish.

After all, they got home early.

How did they do it?

20. After a lengthy trip to the bank, two friends are arguing over whose the bags of money belong to. The two men realize that what they brought is a fortune and so go to court to solve the matter.

The first man tells the judge: "The camel that my friend and I bought carried these bags back to our house. It took me 3 hours to plan for everything! I looked for the right camel, the right time of day, and even which bank we should go."

The second man tells the judge: "I also planned for everything! I called the bank and spoke to the bank teller. I bought the bags to put the money there, and I even fed the camel and gave him water so that he doesn't get tired."

After hearing all of their arguments, the judge, being a wise man, tells the man that the one who carried the bags is the one who will have the money.

Who will have the bags of money?

21. Baxter was the tallest dog in the village. Their owners are very happy that their dog gets a lot of attention. They take good care of him all the time. They bathe him when he's dirty, they take him to the vet when he's sick, and they feed him when he's hungry.

    A competition is organized to determine who the tallest dog is. If Baxter is the tallest dog, then he'll surely win the competition easily. Unfortunately, by the time the competition is over, Baxter loses and becomes the second tallest dog. But... why?

22. One day, Alice asks John:

    "If I gave you two soccer balls, and then two other soccer balls, how many soccer balls would you have?"

    John replies: I would have 5

    Alice says: "No, John. If I have two soccer balls, and then you give me two more soccer balls, how many would I have?"

    To which John replies: "4."

    "That's right. Now, if I gave you 2 soccer balls, and then other 2 soccer balls, how many would you have?"

    John replies: "5."

    It seems that John is wrong, but actually, he isn't. Why can we say that?

23. A farmer wants to leave his inheritance to his 5 children. After dividing everything he has into equal parts, he realizes that the house where he lives hasn't been given to anyone yet.

Since there are 5 children, it will be hard to divide equally among his kids, so he devises a plan. He calls his children and gives each one a seed to plant and tells them that they need to plant each seed. At the end of the year, he will check how good each one of his children took care of the plant.

After a year, the farmer tells his children to show him their plants. Four of them are in front of him, showing him how large their plant has grown, even showing them some fruits that the plants have produced. But the last one is standing on a corner, a little sad because his plant never grew, so he only has the seed to show his father.

When the fifth child's turn comes, the farmer is surprised but decides to give his house to him.

Why did the farmer decide to give his house to the fifth child?

24. At a company, workers are expected to know the password to their personal computers. This password changes every six months, so some of them might easily forget that they need a new password.

One of them goes to his supervisor and asks him what the new password is. His supervisor tells him: "The old password is out of date."

To which the workers said: "I already know that. What's the new password?"

The supervisor goes on to tell him: "The new password is different."

The worker, getting a little frustrated, tells his supervisor: "It's obvious that the new password is different than the

old one, but I need to know the new password."
His supervisor tells him that he has already told him the right password. What's the password the worker has to use, and what was the old password?

25. At a competition, two horsemen are given the chance to win a million dollars. There's only just one condition: to win; they have to finish last. After a couple of hours trying not to cross the line, they stop for a minute and go to their trainers for advice.

    After having consulted with their trainers for some minutes, the men rush to the horses and resume the race as fast as they can.

    What was the advice that their trainers gave them?

26. A father asks his kids to have one of the rooms of the house filled with whatever they can buy with just a couple of dollars. After a while, the first son buys a bed, but it isn't big enough to fill the room.

    The second one buys a flat-screen TV, but it isn't large enough to fill the room. Finally, the third one buys two very cheap and easy-to-find things that completely fill the room. What did the third son buy?

27. A kid enters a candy shop in the mall that's near the airport. After buying all the candies he wishes to eat, the manager of the store tells him that he can take all of those candies home for free if he passes a simple test.

    The manager has one bag in each of his hands. Inside each bag, there's one candy. The manager tells the kid that he has to draw one of the candies from one of the bags. If the candy he chooses is black, then he can take everything for free; but if it's red, he'll have to pay double for all his candies.

    The kid knows that the manager has put read candies in

both bags, but he still accepts the deal. In the end, he wins and doesn't pay for his candies. How did he do it?

28. A couple is on a week-long vacation on a cruise. Unfortunately, the cruise sunk, and every single person on the cruise died. This cruise accident is all over the news. All the newspapers report that every single person died in that terrible accident.

    Amazingly, you see the couple walking on the streets of the city without any problem. How's that possible?

29. A person is trying to enter a party. The security guard tells him that if he wants to enter, he will have to say something that is neither true or false. Also, if the guard thinks that what he has said is true, then the guard will not let him in. if the guard thinks that what he has said is false, then he'll be let in but then immediately kicked out of the party.

    In the end, the man enters the party without any problem, leaving the guard thinking about what he said. What did the man say?

30. Carl needs to enter his class but can't find his classroom. He's told his class is on the fourth floor. When he finally finds the fourth floor, he sees that there are two classrooms that have the same door. Carl knows very well that he can't interrupt the class. Thankfully, there's an exchange student that's also outside with him that can help him find the right classroom. Unfortunately, the exchange student doesn't know how to speak English, but he can understand English. What two yes-or-no questions can Carlos ask the exchange student to find the right classroom?

12

FIENDISH RIDDLES

1. A man is trying to cross to the other side of a river. After a while, he finds two bridges that are guarded by two identical twins. One of the bridges is in perfect condition while the other is about to fall down.

   If he wants to cross, he will have to talk to the brothers and ask them which one is the good bridge. One of them always tells the truth, and the other ones always lie. He only has one chance to ask them.

   So, what question should the man ask?

2. During the day of his execution, a power outage occurs, and the prisoner in question is led to a room where he will live his last moments. He's bee given the opportunity to choose the method of execution.

   He is shown an electric chair and a crocodile. Which method does the man have to choose to survive?

3. After the bank was robbed, the police tried to look for suspects. After searching for quite a while, they have narrowed it to only 3 suspects. They know that only of the suspects always tells the truth.

   After the suspects are questioned, the reply:

   A: I didn't rob the bank!

B: I didn't rob the bank!

C: Suspect B did it!

The police know that suspect B is the only one who tells the truth. In the end, the police arrest the criminal.

Who's robbed the bank?

4. One of Jimmy's uncles is very funny and is always pranking Jimmy. One day, after having lunch, Jimmy's uncle tells him:

   "If I can write your exact age, I'll give you 20 dollars; if I can't do it, you'll give me 20 dollars."

   Realizing that his uncle hasn't visited for a long while and doesn't know much about the family, Jimmy accepts.

   In the end, Jimmy ends up giving his uncle 20 dollars.

5. There are many portraits hanging on one of the walls of Jimmy's school. The teachers tell Jimmy that each portrait is of every president that has ever been elected.

   Jimmy knows a lot of history and knows very well that there have been only 20 presidents, and yet he sees that there are only 19 portraits hanging on the wall.

   What seems to be the problem?

6. Hannah was walking a dog in the forest when she realized that she had lost her purse. After searching for a while, she realized that someone must've stolen her purse. She calls the police, and they arrest 3 suspects.

   The first suspect is a thin, blonde woman who's wearing a white T-shirt and high heels. The second suspect is a very fat man who's wearing dirty boots and a red T-shirt. The last suspect doesn't have many clothes on; he's only got his sandals on and a black shirt.

   Who's the one who robbed Hannah's purse?

7. You see 3 boys, John, Robert, and Charles, waiting outside of a clothing store. They're waiting for the store to open so that they can take advantage of the Black Friday

discounts. These 3 boys have been waiting for a long time until, finally, the door of this store opens.

Who will get the cellphone first? John, Robert, or Charles?

8. You are the nurse in a hospital. You see that, during the morning, there were 3 women and 2 guys who were helped. In the afternoon, there are 2 guys and no women who were helped. Finally, at night, there are 8 women, 2 guys and 5 children who were helped. And just before your shift ends, one more woman is helped. How old is the nurse?

9. As you were sleeping, all your family came over as a surprise. They have brought many gifts for you. Your mom has brought some new clothes, your dad has brought some nice videogames, and your brother has brought a new bicycle. All of these are wrapped, what do you open first?

10. On a rainy day, a woman enters a bar and orders a beer. Realizing she is sitting next to a rich man, she proposes a challenge. She tells the rich kan that she can sing a song that includes any word ever said.

   "Impossible," says the rich man, "You would have to know all songs ever recorded."

   The woman tells the rich man that she indeed knows every song in the world. She further tells him that if he can come up with the most difficult word or phrase a song can include and she's able to sing it, then he should give her one thousand dollars.

   Incredulous and thinking that he has nothing to lose, the man accepts. For a couple of minutes, the mane tries to come up with a very difficult word but seems to be unable to do so. Finally, the rich man thinks that the name of her dog is difficult enough and so rare that no song no

Earth has ever mentioned it.

In the end, the woman gets out of the bar with one thousand dollars.

What did the woman sing to win those thousand dollars?

11. Two kids are trying to escape their school. Unfortunately, a huge wall surrounds their school. The only exit seems to be the window that is 20 meters above the ground.

    One of the kids, realizing how difficult it would be to get out of the school through that window, tells the other kid to escape through a hole they can dig below the ground. The other kid thinks it's a good plan and so agrees.

    After many hours of digging bricks and dirt, they realize that they're getting nowhere and so devise another plan to escape.

    How do they escape?

12. George and Francis used to be friends, but now don't get along very well. One day, George helps a lost man who has been robbed. This man is very rich and tells him that he will get 3 things he asks for.

    The only condition is that Francis will receive half of everything that George asks for. George agrees and starts to think about what he will ask first.

    After thinking deeply for a minute, he first asks for two million dollars. Without any hassle, the rich man writes a check for George and hands it to him. George can hardly believe it, but he has received two million dollars. Also, the rich man writes another check for Francis. Francis' check is of one million dollars.

    Even though he doesn't want Francis to also receive any money, he understands the condition. Without thinking too much about it, he now asks for a huge mansion in a very nice area of the city. The rich man accepts, and he gives George a beautiful country house, but he also gives

Francis half a mansion.

George is angry at this but can't complain. Trying to devise a plan to get all that Francis is also getting, he utters his final request. The rich man complies, and, on the next day, Francis is found dead.

What did George ask for as his last request?

13. On his way to the mall after an exhausting day of school, John sees his chemistry teacher. This teacher reminds John of the homework he left two days ago. He says goodbye to him and continues walking. A little while later, he sees some of his classmates. There are eight of them, and each one carries their own bag. Finally, he spots a guy with his girlfriend. This guy's girlfriend has a bag and inside the bag, John can clearly see that there are 2 bottles of water.

    How many people are going to the mall?

14. A farmer comes up to you and tells you that his cow has been walking for many miles without getting tired. Trying to measure for how long and how much they walk, the farmer puts a device on the four legs of the cow.

    The farmer finds out that his cow usually walks for 5 hours without stopping. That's not the only fascinating fact, but, on a normal day, 2 legs of the cow walk for 80 kilometers, and the other 2 legs of the cow walk for 81 kilometers.

    You know that's not possible, and the cow and the device are perfectly normal. So what seems to be the problem?

15. One college student is asked by his teacher to tell him a riddle about time. The teacher tells the students to find the time when the hands of the clock are perfectly aligned, but at the same time, these hands have to be exactly between the numbers one and two.

    How does the college student respond?

16. I have 10 glass bottles that I have drunk with my school friends, and now I have a lot I can use to play.

    If I place the bootles in some order, I can make them touch a certain number of bottles. What would be the minimum amount of bottles I need to place so that every bottle touches exactly 3 bottles?

17. A boy named Alex is at the stadium. He tries to buy a cap from the gift shop that's outside the stadium. Unfortunately, he only has a $50 bill. No one at the gift shop has change.

    One of the employees at the gift shop takes Alex's bill and tells him that he will ask another shopper if he has change. After asking a couple of them, the employee finds a woman who is willing to change the $50 bill.

    Alex buys the cap. The cap cost $15. The employee gives Alex his change: $35.

    After a while, the woman that changed the bill for the employee and Alex come back to the gift shop complaining that the bill is counterfeit. She demands her money back, and so the gift shop gives her money back.

    How much money did the gift shop lose?

18. Inside a house, there's a whole family that's trying to make good use of their time since there's been a power outage.

    The family is made up of the father, the mother, the grandfather, the grandmother, two sons, and one daughter, and you.

    Trying to know what they are doing, you begin to look for them and see that the father is talking to the mother. They seem to be having a good conversation since they have been talking for over an hour now.

    Next, you look for the grandmother. You see that the grandmother is in the garden planting some plants and cutting some of them. the grandfather is also helping her; he's raking the leaves that have fallen to the ground and putting them into a plastic bag.

Finally, you see that one of the sons is playing chess while the daughter is washing the dishes.

What's the other son doing?

19. On a plane, there are 15 people. Those 15 include pilots, flight attendants, and passengers. What they don't know is that there's one more that's infiltrated the plane.

    This person tries to hijack the plane. After successfully taking everything he wanted from the passengers, he plans on escaping by jumping out of the plane. To do this, the highjacker asks for 16 parachutes.

    Without hesitation, the passengers give the highjacker the 16 parachutes he's asking for. After putting one of them on, he jumps out of the plane and leaves behind all the other parachutes.

    Why did the highjacker leave the other parachutes?

20. A taxi driver is on his way to the city center. He's on a one-way street, and he's going in the wrong direction. Still, nobody says anything and the police don't stop him.

    On his way back home, he takes another route. The streets where he's is also a one-way street one. He's also going in the wrong direction. Even though it's pretty obvious, the police don't stop him.

    When asked why they didn't stop the man, they answered that the man didn't break any law.

    How's that possible if the man was going in the wrong direction all the time?

21. At an Italian racetrack, all local newspapers are reporting about the horse race that's going to take place in just a couple of minutes. In this race, 1 Italian rider and 1

American rider are going to participate.

The local media is obviously biased. They have been saying how the Italian rider has more experience, has won more races than the American, and how the horse is stronger than the one the American is going to ride.

After a couple of minutes, the race begins. At first, it seems like the Italian horse is going to win the race, but in the end, the American horse wins the race.

Sad and a little angry, the local media refuse to publish or report the race in a way that gives the impression that the Italian lost.

How do they publish a headline without making it obvious that the Italian lost?

22. Every time a man needs to buy ingredients to make lunch, he goes to the local supermarket. He loves eating spaghetti and would love to eat them every day. Unfortunately, he can only buy spaghetti on rainy days. Every other day, he buys whatever other ingredients he can find.

    Since there's always spaghetti available at the supermarket, why can't he buy them any other days and not just on rainy days?

23. At a local fast food restaurant, there's a clown that likes picking up on people and prank them. This time, the clown offers a deal you can't refuse.

    The clown shows you a large table. On that large table, there are 6 glasses, three of which are filled to the brim with soda. They are in a row, though. The first 3 glasses are filled, and the other 3 are empty.

    The clown tells you to move one of the glasses filled with soda so that now the empty glasses and the full glasses alternate.

Which of the three glasses do you move to alternate them?

24. At a grocery store, you see that there are a lot of vegetables and fresh fruits. Unfortunately, some of the pears are rotten. To make matters worse, you cannot tell which pear is good and which one isn't.

    But you don't have to worry. The seller tells you that you can weigh the pears, and then you'll know which one is rotten. She tells you that the rotten one weighs much less and that the good ones all weigh the same.

    There are nine pears in front of you, and one of them is rotten. You also have the scale for yourself, but just for some minutes. You want to take 8 pears home but don't want to take the one that is rotten. You also don't want to stay there for a long while.

    What's the minimum amount of times you need to weigh the pears to exactly know which is the rotten one?

25. An old woman that's been married for 30 years is seen shooting her husband inside the house they've been living since they got married. The shot was quick and without much noise. After a while, the woman is also seen keeping her beloved husband underwater for 5 minutes. Finally, the old woman hangs the husband. Just 10 minutes later, her husband and her go out for a walk.

    How can this possible?

26. After shopping at a mall near the airport, a father and a son are getting back home. Unfortunately, an accident occurs, and both the father and the child are injured. Some minutes later, the father dies while the boy is rushed to the hospital as soon as possible so that he can get the medical help he needs.

    Upon entering the hospital, the surgeon looks at the boy

and says: "I can't operate this boy. He's my son."
How's that possible?

27. Can you decipher the message behind these words? :
Yetti or university
Ant rabbit elephant
Apple
Great original ordeal defunct
Reason intelligent day dove lost esteem
Sinus obese love ear ruin

28. As you're walking through the local market, you see a man that has an ad that says:
- You can buy 1 for just one dollar
- You can buy 10 for just 2 dollars
- You can buy 100 for just 3 dollars
A woman approaches the man and then tells him that she want 917. The man gives her 917 but only charges her 3 dollars,
How's that possible?

29. Your local town hall has enacted a strange law. As you can see it in the newspaper, this new law says that every man living in San Francisco cannot be buried in L.A.
Why is this law enacted?

30. The recently graduated college student is happy because he's gotten his first interview. He has always wanted to become an engineer and now has the chance to be one.
At the job interview, he's asked many questions about his studies and how his grades. Since he has never worked before as an engineer, the interviewer wants to make sure he's hiring the right person.
In order to prove that the man has creativity and that he's not afraid to think outside the box, the interviewer asks him what seems to be a simple question:
"I dropped an egg to the ground from 20 meters high and

yet it didn't crack or break, how's that possible?"

What's the answer to the interviewer's question?

31. Four friends are participating in a dog contest. This contest takes place every year in December to know who's the best and most obedient dog in town. Every contestant is allowed to bring two dogs of any breed they want. At the contest, there are many dogs, and the four friends have 2 dogs, each enrolled in the competition. The breeds of the dogs the four friends have are Labrador, Bulldog, Husky, and Chow Chow. Interestingly, no friend has two dogs of the same breed and there are only two dogs of each breed.

    Roxanne doesn't have a Chow Chow. Manny doesn't have a Labrador, but he has a Bulldog. One of them has a Chow Chow and a Husky and another friend has a Bulldog and a Husky. Donald has a Chow Chow. Brad has a Husky but he doesn't have a Bulldog.

    As a judge, you need to know which dog belongs to whom. Do you know which friend has which dogs?

32. A grandmother and her granddaughter are about to leave the house for the supermarket. As they leave, they forget to take her grandson with them, too.

    Both the grandmother and the granddaughter are on a bus that is going at 30 km/h. The grandson knows that he won't be able to reach them if he goes to the supermarket on foot because he can only walk at 15 km/h. The grandson then decides to ride his bike to the supermarket since he can ride his bike at 25 km/h.

    As he's riding his bike, he doesn't make any turn and doesn't reduce his speed.

    How far will he go in an hour?

33. Dave's watch is broken, and he needs to fix it. He asks his grandfather for help since he's been fixing watches since

he's a teenager. As Dave's grandfather is working to fix the watch, he asks Dave a very interesting riddle and tells him that if he's able to solve it, he won't need to pay anything for having fixed his watch, but if he can't solve it, he will need to pay his grandfather.

Dave accepts the challenge. His grandfather proceeds to tell him:

"Time is important everywhere; we need to be punctual wherever we go. Sometimes, time is all we need to solve our problems, as in this riddle. The clock can only count to 12, but time goes beyond that. Time should be counted like this:

100-365-12-54-7-24-60-60"

What do these numbers represent?

34. During summer vacation, Roxanne is told to go to the doctor. She obviously doesn't want to go until her vacation is over, but her parents tell her that she has to go, or she will be grounded.

    One of the friends comes up with a very good idea. She asks Roxanne when her vacation is over. "In a week," Roxanne tells her friend.

    So her friend goes to the grocery store and buys 7 apples. When she sees Roxanne again, she gives her the seven apples she purchased.

    Why did Roxanne's friend do this?

35. Trying to make math fun, the math teacher at John's school come up with a very interesting math riddle. He asks his students to tell him their names and so, he says:

    "Jennifer is 15

    Mark is 5

    Richard is 10

    Danny is 5

    Francisco is 15

And Angelina is 20"

The students are puzzled since they know very well that he's not talking about their ages. No one in class is 5 or 20!

The teacher goes on to say:

"How much, then, is Dominic?

36. A woman is trying to get his barrel full of wine transported on a boat across the river. This barrel weighs more than 250 kilograms. Unfortunately, the barrel cannot be transported on the boat that she has since it's too heavy. She tries to put his barrel on another boat, but she still finds that the barrel is too heavy to be transported on a boat. Being rejected after asking many people if they are willing o transport the barrel, she finally gives up.

Just before sundown, a man, who is an experienced sailor, approaches the woman and accepts to transport the barrel on his boat across the river. The woman, incredulous at first, asks the sailor:

"How can you transport the barrel of it's too heavy?"

The sailor responded:

"It doesn't matter if the barrel weighs 100, 200, or more kilograms. I can put something on the barrel that will make it lose some weight?"

What's the sailor going to put on the barrel?

37. After walking for a couple of miles to find the nearest town, two men finally find a spot where they can get some rest. They've been walking in the desert for many hours without end. They are very tired.

These men attract everyone's attention since they seem to be foreigners; they are wearing different clothes and have different hairstyles. When asked what they are doing in town, they answer that there was an accident and that they are the only survivors of the accident.

At first, the townspeople don't believe him:

"We see that you guys have your backpacks open. We assume that you are robbers that have come to our town to steal."

The two respond:

"We are not robbers. Our backpacks are open because we survived. Those who died didn't have their backpacks open."

The townspeople try to get to the bottom of the mystery and go to search for the missing men who died in the accident. As the two men said, those who are dead don't have their backpacks open.

The townspeople can't believe what happened.

What did the two men have in their backpacks?

38. John goes on a trip to New York City to visit his favorite author. The name of this author is Ryan. After talking to Ryan for a whole day, John finds out that he's trying to finish a new book.

Ryan tells John that this book has taken most of his time and might possibly never be able to finish it. puzzled, John asks Ryan what that book is about.

Ryan doesn't want to tell John what the book is, but he gives him a clue:

"I've been able to finish many, many books in my life, and for that, I'm very grateful. I've written about so many topics that it's hard for me to even count them. But there's a book so long that I've tried to write it almost every day of my life. Still, I know very well that, no matter how long I live, I will never be able to finish it."

John thinks he knows what book Ryan is talking about.

What type of book is Ryan talking about?

39. Many people are trying to answer as many questions as they can in an interview that the local town hall is con-

ducting. It's part of the job fair. These job fairs take place every last day of the month, and this time is no different. Wanting to work at a factory as a chemist, a person walks to a stand and tries to get as much information as possible. He realizes he can have his job interview right on the spot and so he proceeds to have it. After 30 minutes, the chemist is hired and goes to celebrate with his family.

After a couple of minutes, another person approaches the stand and also tries to have a job interview on the spot. He is an engineer that is unemployed. This time, the interviewer notes that the chemist and the engineer might be related since they both have the same last name.

To have his doubts cleared, the interviewer asks the chemist if that chemist has a brother. The chemist says the engineer is his brother. The interviewer then asks the engineer for a brother. The engineer says he doesn't have a brother.

How's that possible?

40. At a clothing store, there are a lot of men who come from far away to buy the best hats they can find. This store has made many hats for many famous people.

It's a custom in this town to take the hat off every time, someone, important, or someone who has a lot of power enters the store. One day, the prime minister came to visit the store. Every man in the store quickly took off their hats when they saw him entering the store.

Another day, a celebrity entered the store. Since some people liked the celebrity and so, they took off their hats. But some didn't, and they didn't take off their hats to the celebrity.

During the weekend, the most powerful men on the nation, the king, came to visit the store. Everyone, including the salesmen, took off their hats. When he was gone, everyman put their hats back on. Wondering to whom the king takes his hat off, they start mentioning names and people that might be even more powerful and important than the king.

One man decides to join the conversation and tell the men in the store that he knows one man in town to whom the king takes his hat off every once in a while. This elderly man tells the others that the man to whom the king takes his hat off isn't very important and that the king is happy to do it every time. Not only that, but he says that every person does exactly that.

Who is the man to whom the king and every other man take their hats off?

41. At a women's social gathering, women are talking about what they do for a living. All of the women know each other very well, and they have been friends for a long time but haven't seen each other for a couple of years now, and so they're trying to catch up with the latest news.

One woman says: "I traveled to Itay three years ago and met my now-husband. He's a great husband. I'm pregnant now, and I think I'm going to give birth in January. I haven't decided his name yet."

Another woman says: "I'm happy for you. My son was born just last year. His name is Daniel. He was born in Michigan, and my husband and I are very happy for him."

A third woman says: "You remind me of the time when I and my husband had our first child. It was a girl, and her name is Rose. She was born 5 years ago."

Finally, the last woman mentions: "My baby is also a newborn. His name is Ian, and he was born in May. The funny thing is that his birthday is in June."

All the women around her look puzzled. How can the last woman's baby be born in May, but his birthday is in June?

42. Dave's friend has come to visit his house. His name is Justin. Daves invites him to play videogames in his living room but realizes that he left his games in his bedroom.

    Justin wants to help him, so he goes upstairs to Dave's room to help him find his videogames. There's no electricity in Dave's room at the moment so they have to look for the games in the dark. While they try to find the games, Dave also tells Justin that he needs to find a T-shirt.

    Daves then tells Justin that there's a drawer that contains all of his T-shirts. Inside that drawer, there are 6 white T-shirts, 3 black T-shirts, 2 red T-shirts, and 5 blue T-shirts. Since Dave wants to take two of the same color, how many would Justin have to pull out from the drawer in the dark to get a matching pair of T-shirts?

43. Nicole is driving home after a long afternoon of shopping at the mall. The roads in the city where Nicole is living are very well maintained, and she loves driving her car. In all honesty, though, she stills remember the times when she used to use public transport.

    Since she's remembering those old times, she decides to pass by a bus stop that's close to the mall. As she gets close to the bus stop, she notices that there's a line not as long as she thought it would be. She also sees 3 people in line that attract her attention.

    The first person is an old man that seems very tired and like he doesn't have much energy to stand up on his feet for very long. The second person is a dear friend of Nicole's. She lives near her house, and they have grown up together, even going to the same high school. Finally, Nicole finds a work colleague. Nicole is in love with this man and they have been dating for a while.

Nicole is a good person and wants to offer a ride to one of the people who are waiting for the bus. The question is: to whom does she offer the ride?

44. Austin's grandparents left him a large inheritance. One of the things he received is a safe that contains many objects of great value like diamonds, golden rings, and checks that he can cash. Even though he's happy to give his grandson all of this, he's afraid that someone might copy the keys he's sending and then try to open the lock. Austin comes up with a very good plan to open the safe without his grandfather, sending him the key right away. What's Austin's plan?

45. Many people are at a great reception at a wedding. They're celebrating and having a good time. After a while, many men and women are a little bit drunk, and so they start to play and dance frantically.

Thankfully, not all of the people at the wedding are behaving that way, but there are two men who seem to be having an argument over the drinks they're getting. The argument is not about the number of drinks they have but about how much is left in the barrel.

One of the hosts decides to settle this argument by showing the two men that there's still a lot of liquor inside the barrel. He claims that the barrel is more than half full. One of the men who was arguing agrees with him while the other strongly disagrees.

It's a party, so they don't have a way to measure if the barrel is half full or not. But the host wants to settle this argument right now. What does he need to do to show the men how full the barrel is?

46. After school, you go to your best friend's house. There, your friend offers to show you the books that she has

read. After being shown the books, you can't help but notice that she lies ordering the books in a certain order. The order of the books is very simple. All of them are in a pile, and they all have 5 different colors: red, blue, orange, pink, and black. She wants to play with you to know if you can remember the color of the books and so she covers your eyes and begins asking you about the books. Of course, you can't remember all the colors, and so she starts giving you some clues. The clues go like this:
  - The name of the color of the book that's at the bottom has 6 letters
  - The pink book is between the red and blue books.
  - The pink book is above the black book but below the blue book.
  - Now your friend wants to know if you can remember the order of the books

47. You're a tourist in a city where there are a lot of skyscrapers. You are staying at a hotel near the center of the city. You find that this hotel is also a skyscraper and has a lot of floors.

As you ask for the key to your room, you find out that the floors in this skyscraper have unusual names. You think that they're messing up with you but realize that this is true the minutes you get on the elevator. When the elevator operator asks you your floor number, you don't really know what to say.

You don't need to worry because the elevator operator wants to help you see how you can find out the name of your floor. He says that the floor one is called the first floor; floor 2 is called the second floor. The fifteenth floor is called "a quarter floor"; the thirtieth floor is called "half floor."

Your floor is 62. What do you call the floor where you're staying?

48. John has a friend who is a professional driver. The name of this professional driver is Francis. Francis has a lot of experience diving; he has been to many parts of the world and has won many diving contests. People all around the country know very well who Francis is. But Francis has a defect. Sometimes, he likes to show off too much. On occasion, he tells his friends, including John, that he can hold his breath for 20 minutes underwater. No one needs to question his ability to do that, but John thinks he can hold his breath even longer. Surprised, everyone tells John to show if he can really do that. John says that he will do it and that, if he's able to pull that off, Francis will have to give him $500. Francis accepts, and so John starts to show it. Keep in mind that John doesn't have any experience diving but still manages to win the $500. How was he able to do that?

49. At a state fair, there are many people who have come from many places to enjoy a good time with their families and friends. Some of them try to collect the prizes that are available to everyone. Alexander tries to collect one of the prizes, too. A clown is offering a teddy bear to whoever is able to solve his riddle. The clown has thirty combs and two bags. Half of the thirty combs are blue, and the other half is red. He says that he will give the prize if the person put all the combs in the two bags. That sounds easy, doesn't it? But continues. The clown says that he has to put his hand inside a bag and draw a red comb from any bag. But if the comb he draws from the bab is blue, then the contest will have lost. Alexander accepts the challenge. The clown only tells him that

no bag has to be empty and that all the combs have to be used. What does he need to do to get the prize?

50. Sophie is painting her room with the help of her friends. Even though she needs to study for her finals exam, she still manages to completely paint her room. One of her friends who helped her paint her room, Maria, wants to take some paint that was left to her house. Sophie lets her take some paint buckets. When Maria finally gets home, she starts painting her own room with the same paint. Out of nowhere, her brother interrupts her and starts asking what color is the one she's using to paint her room. "It's easy," she says. "What is yellow but smells like blue paint?" Do you know the answer?

13

ANSWERS FOR FUN RIDDLES

1. A platypus
2. A bicycle with training wheels
3. You can get the police's attention faster if you commit a crime
4. You need to wash them with black clothes
5. Glasses
6. The credits
7. Superheroes have superpowers
8. Smart people
9. Yellowstone
10. A baby
11. Any hand. It doesn't matter which hand as long as you know how to write.
12. There are a lot of bats
13. They wave you when you see them
14. Because they can always smell a carrot
15. Because he keeps getting holes in one
16. Because his heart isn't in it.

14

ANSWERS FOR DIFFICULT RIDDLES

1. You need to count yourself
2. A dog is pregnant for a little more than 3 months. After 9 months, you get more puppies than usual.
3. You forgot to count the bus driver's seat
4. They all would have to speak a language the mayor can understand. Since it's New York City's mayor we're talking about, the answer is English.
5. He read for 15 minutes but had to stay some minutes more to speak to the librarian.
6. That's the order of the musical notes.
7. A piano
8. A mon-key
9. An adult
10. All months have 28 days
11. A sea lion
12. He's listening
13. Traffic lights
14. A towel

15. To know the answer to this, you need to take a look at the flags from Iceland and Norway. You can see that both are similar, the only difference being the color. Knowing this difference, you can now understand how he was able to find out to whom the wallet belonged to.
16. They need to have children first.
17. The child is adopted. Since the device can only detect inherited illnesses, it's obvious that nothing can be found within the child.
18. At first, the answer might seem to be half the number what the guard says. The answer actually is the number of letters every number has.
19. All the children at school need to plan ahead. They need to agree on someone who won't show the book while the others will.
20. The one who carried the bags will get the money, that is, the camel.
21. If you read carefully the first sentence, you'll see that he **was.** He's not the tallest dog anymore.
22. He's not wrong. He's already got one at home.
23. The father gave all the kids fake seeds that wouldn't sprout or give any fruit. The only one who was honest enough was the last son. All the other ones replaced the fake seeds with real ones.
24. The old password was "out of date." The new password is "different."
25. They were advised to switch horses.
26. A candle and a match. When the candle is lighted, its aroma fills the room.
27. He eats one of the candy. After eating, he asks what's inside of the other bag. Since the other bag has a red candy, he can say that the other one must've been a black one.

28. Only single people died in the accident. They were a couple.
29. I'll be kicked out of the party.“Is this the class?” and then he can ask, “Yes?”

15

ANSWERS FOR FIENDISH RIDDLES

1. The question would be: "Which one would your brother use?"
2. An electric chair since there's no electricity.
3. A did it. C is reinforcing the idea that B didn't rob the bank.
4. He just wrote "exact age" on the paper.
5. One of the presidents had to serve 2 terms
6. The second one. Remember that Hannah was in the forest, and the second suspect has his shoes very dirty.
7. No one. It's a clothing store, not a cell phone store.
8. As old as you are since you're the nurse.
9. Your eyes
10. Happy birthday
11. The put all the dirt in a pile and then climb it until they reach the window.
12. Beat me until I'm half dead.
13. Just John. He's the only one on his way to the mall.
14. The cow is walking in circles. The "inner legs," which are two, are waling less than the "outer legs."

15. 12 is the right number.

16. 4

17. $50

18. He's playing chess, too. Remember that 2 people are needed to play chess.

19. He wanted to fool everyone that he was going to jump out of the plane with the hostages. Had he asked for only one parachute, the passengers may have given him a defective one.

20. He's walking

21. The American horse came next to last.

22. He's short. He needs an umbrella to reach the top shelves at the store.

23. Pour what's inside the second glass into the fifth.

24. Just twice. First, put all the pears in 3 piles. And then, weigh two of them on the scale. Surely, one of the pears is the rotten one because you'll see that one pile is heavier than the other. And if that's not the case, then the rotten pear is in the third pile. If that's the case, then you can weigh the pears in that pile to know which one is the rotten one.

25. The woman is a photographer. She took a shot of her husband that she was taking a picture of her husband. Then, she developed, and, finally, he hung the picture to dry it.

26. The surgeon is the mother of the boy.

27. YOU ARE A GREAT RIDDLE SOLVER

28. Those are house numbers. Three house numbers are just 3 dollars

29. Because you cannot bury a living man

30. The floor didn't crack

31. Roxanne has a Labrador and a Bulldog. Manny has a Bulldog and a Husky. Donald has a Chow Chow and a Labrador. Brad has a Husky and a Chow Chow.

32. 25 kilometers because he can ride his bike at 25 km/hr.

33. 100 is the number of years in a century. 365 is the number of days in a year. 12 is the number of months in a year. 52 is the number of weeks in a year. 7 is the number of days in a week. 24 is the number of hours in a day. 60 is the number of minutes of an hour. 60 is also the number of seconds in a minute.

34. She gives her 7 apples because "an apple a day keeps the doctor away."

35. 15. Each syllable equals 5.

36. A hole

37. Parachutes. Since their parachutes opened, they are alive. The other didn't have their parachutes opened and so couldn't survive.

38. An autobiography

39. The chemist is the engineer's sister

40. the hairdresser

41. May is the name of the place where the kid was born

42. Five. Four times to pick one of all the colors and one more to get the matching pair.

43. She offers the old man a ride and gives the keys to her best. Then, she gets out of her car to wait for the bus with her work colleague.

44. The grandson receives the safe with his grandfather's lock. The grandson receives the safe, but he puts a lock of his own on it and gives it back to his grandfather. The grandfather receives the safe with the two locks, his and his grandson's; he unlocks his own lock and gives it one more time to his grandson. The grandson receives it for

one last time and sees that the only lock there is his, so he opens it.

45. He straightens the barrel and opens it to see if it's half full or not.
46. Blue, pink, red, black, and orange.
47. One minute floor because it's "sixty-one."
48. He held a glass of water above his head for 30 minutes.
49. Fills one bag with only red combs and leaves the other with only blue ones.
50. Yellow paint.

3

HARD RIDDLES

16

THANKSGIVING RIDDLES

1. There are so many of us at thanksgiving. But people do not want to see us wasted. Our meat is extremely juicy, but we have to be basted first.
2. I am a starchy type of food. Sometimes I am mashed and fried at other times. I am mostly found in Idaho and live underground until people dig me out. Who am I?
3. It is a very popular grain, yellow in color and grows outside in fields. Once the husk is peeled and done cooking, most people prefer to add some butter on it.
4. They were the first people ever to celebrate thanksgiving many years back in the 1600s. The people back then wore black and white clothes and very funny hats. Who were they?
5. After every serving of turkey on Thanksgiving, most people look forward to enjoying this fruit as it helps fill the belly. Sometimes, the fruit is served as a sauce or jelly at other times.

6. This is one of those dishes that people love to chew down because it is a very tasty side dish. It is prepared using marshmallows, sweet potatoes and brown sugar.

7. It is a sport that is traditionally watched during thanksgiving. Every year, people sit down during thanksgiving and watch two popular teams the Lions and Cowboys play against each other on the fields.

8. The image of this brings out the best fall picture. It has all the season's harvest and is a horn.

9. It is something that you grow but it sounds like a month. It is also a ship that pilgrims used.

10. It is orange in color and baked in a pie. You can spy on your little eye.

11. Roses are red, violets are blue. What is brown and blue and is always stuffed?

12. Sometimes I am hot and other times cold. Sometimes, I am prepared with fruits, sometimes vegetables and other times meat. Whatever way people chose to make me, I am always a big treat on Thanksgiving table, perhaps the best treat ever. Who am I?

13. On this day, there is a festive event along all the streets. Bugs Bunny, Felix, Dora and Mickey join everyone else and make way for it. What event is this?

14. I have flakes, but I do not have hair. I have ears but I cannot hear. Any idea who I am?

15. What is the common between Pilgrims, Indians and Puritans?

16. The duck, goose, turkey, chicken and peasant all got into trouble. What did they do?

17. No matter what happens, you can never eat me on Thanksgiving Dinner. It does not matter how rich you are, once it is thanksgiving dinner you cannot have me.

18. Grateful, joyful, thankful and wonderful all have something in common.
19. More than any other sides, this side of the turkey has more feathers. Which is this side?
20. It is very big, usually brown and red all over.
21. Sometimes a turkey can have three legs even if turkeys have only two. How is this possible?
22. What distinguishes the turkey from a chicken?
23. Imagine you are carving a turkey with an electric cutter. Then suddenly, power goes off before you are through. What battery will you use on the cutter as a substitute?
24. It has feathers and a beak, but it is also dressed up.
25. Which part of the turkey is its left side?
26. On Thanksgiving Day, I get stuffed and dressed up. Who am I?
27. Who can fly higher, an ostrich or a turkey?
28. The pilgrims walked off their boat away from them, into a new world. But what did they stand on?
29. It has feathers, a bowed head and kneels. What is it?
30. What do you think the pumpkin whispered to the turkey?
31. On Halloween we get scared, on Christmas Day we feel jolly, but what do we feel on Thanksgiving Day?
32. I am not a nun and neither am I a priest. However, I wear black and white clothes plus very funny hats. I was also an adventurer.
33. April showers bring us May flowers. What do May flowers bring us?
34. It is hard, has an odd shape and is said to bring you good fortune every Thanksgiving. What is it?
35. A tur-key has a key, a don-key has a key. So what does a monkey have?

36. What do you do if you want to see a Pilgrim and a turkey float?

37. It has feathers, is wild and always very ready for a party.

38. As long as it is Thanksgiving Day, you will see me everywhere. They dress me up and though I badly want to get away, I can no longer fly.

39. The turkey was arrested and jailed. Who knows why?

40. Pumpkins and gourds have a favorite sport, which is it?

41. Try to cross a turkey and a monkey, what do you get?

42. Three women take four hours to roast a turkey. How many hours will four women take to fully roast the same turkey?

43. Four women take four hours to bake four pumpkin pies. How many pies can eight women bake in eight hours?

44. The turkey ended up all dressed in the oven and was already killed. What happened?

45. How do you tell apart a female turkey from a male turkey?

46. It is red and covered all over by feathers.

47. Some people love me as an apple; some love me as a sweet potato. Some prefer me warm, while others like me cold.

48. Sometimes Christmas comes before Thanksgiving. When is that rare time when this happens?

49. A turkey goes Gooble! Gooble! Gooble! Then a peach goes Cobbler! Cobbler!cobbler! so what will a computer say?

50. Everything on this list belongs to the Thanksgiving table. Which one is the odd one out and why? Onions, Carrots, Apples and Sweet potatoes

51. We came over in Mayflowers, we sailed the oceans using a ship that was assisted by wind power. We never knew how to grow crops, but we were taught along the way and became excellent farmers. Who were we?

52. it is a tasty bird that flies through the air. It is a Thanksgiving delicacy. What bird is this?

53. I am a 12-letter word and have two compound words. In fall, everyone celebrates me.

54. I am a special kind of key because I can fly and gobble. Who do you think I am?

55. It is big, brown and is stuffed.

56. It goes up and down and has a lot of feathers. In November festivities, the day cannot be complete without it.

57. A pear, an apple and a peach all come from a tree. Where does a turkey come from?

58. Sometimes it is crushed, other times it is baked, while other times it is carved. You cannot miss it on Thanksgiving Day. What is it?

59. What weather is most likely to rain down turkeys and birds?

60. What is a mathematician's favorite delicacy on Thanksgiving Day?

17

CUTE RIDDLES FOR KIDS

1. I am a flying creature and very colorful, but no, I am not a rainbow. I am a very social creature and I know I am very beautiful, but I am not a human being. Who am I?
2. She is very beautiful and very famous. She is very flexible and can be anything you want her to be. People of different tastes will go after her because she can be different and fit for everyone's taste. She knows people have different tastes, so she comes with different colors and different sizes. Sometimes, she has long hair while other times she has short hair. Sometimes she is a blonde while other times she is a brunette. She can rock straight or curly hair and comfortably fit in your hands. Who is she?
3. I am very soft and cuddly, though I look like am grizzly sometimes. Sometimes, I am very big while other times I am just a tiny thing you can hold in your hands. Whatever the size you chose me, I am always stuffed and ready to cuddle you. What am I?
4. We love jumping from one plant into another. Sometimes we are very loud and yes, noisy as we make our

buzz and bumbling sounds. We give you something very sweet that you all love, but we are not always very friendly. Who are we?

5. I am a very stubborn creature who loves jumping from one tree to another. I have a long tail that I love to swing back and forth with whenever I am thinking of something serious. My favorite meals are fruits, nuts and some certain types of seeds. I have some features of a human being, but I am not one. What am I?

6. How did the tiger feel after eating Ellen De Generes and Jimmy Kimmel?

7. if farts are yellow, what do you think is the color of your burps?

8. They live in houses as pets. It is said that they have more lives than any other creature. They are fluffy and sometimes want to be cuddled, while other times they just want to be left alone. They can be super active or super lazy. What are they?

9. They can swim as well as fish, and are slow as turtles. They hang and live on trees like monkeys. Who are they?

10. Sometimes it is a girl, other times it is a boy. Sometimes, it is porcelain while other times it is plastic. But, it is always a toy that you can play with.

11. My home is in the wild. I am always in black and white make-up. Sometimes, I have patterns, prints and stripes. What am I?

12. I am the boss of the flock because I am big, tall and very strong. I can also run very fast. I have wings as well but sadly, I cannot fly. Who am I?

13. It is a beast that is believed to have just one horn. I am mystical and, therefore, very difficult to catch. You know me?

14. What in the world can be half of an elephant?

15. Almost everyone loves me. Some love me, but cannot have me since they get allergies from my fur. Those that do not have allergies have me in their houses because I am very friendly. I love sitting by the window at home so that I can watch who comes in and who leaves. When I am excited, I like wagging a certain part of my body. What am I?

16. They are very colorful flowers and have a beautiful fragrance. They also have little ones. What type are they?

17. He flies around with bows and arrows. However, when he makes shots, he does no harm. Instead of pain, all you feel is a lot of joy. Who is this guy?

18. At times it is hot, other times it is either sweet or better. Some people love it when it is given to them as a gift. It comes in different shapes of blocks, chips and bars. Other times it is just a fountain that you can dip. What is it?

19. It's very fancy and very shiny. Every girl, young and old, wants to have it. It is a perfect gift idea from a boy that really likes a girl. What is it?

20. Most girls cannot go out without it. It makes them feel more beautiful. It is something that you apply on your body, lips and face.

21. You and your girlfriend went out on a date. She is under an umbrella, but you are not. However, you do not get rained on. How is that possible?

22. It is circular and the bigger it is, the better the girls love it. It can be silver or gold but is always very shiny. Boys give them to their girls as a sign of commitment. To do so, the boy goes down on one knee and slides it on a girl's finger.

23. What excites girls when they watch Bridesmaids, Mermaids, Pretty Woman and Legally Blonde?

24. It does not matter how young or how old they are. It does not matter if they are either steady or broken. They are very protective and caring and can do anything for the ones they love. Who are they?

25. I am crushed, I am thrashed, I am clogged and I am also given or kept. Whatever I go through, I always remain the same, I am always whole.

26. It can be a quick one or a little long. It can be given as the first or even as the last one. It can be given at any time by very special people in your life. It is weird, but also weirdly sweet. What is it?

27. I can be found on the internet or the newspaper or even a calendar. I can be rather expensive, but can also be cheap and affordable. I can be a treat for someone special. You can have me in the park, a movie theatre or even a restaurant. However, you have to be two to enjoy me. Who am I?

28. Every girl enjoys a regular treat of this. I come in red, yellow and pink colors. I smell very nice but sometimes when you pick me you have to be very careful or I will bite you. Who am I?

29. I may be cracked, sometimes chapped and even pale. However, there is one thing that is always constant; am always very soft, full and sometimes red. I am always shared between special people. Sometimes, with strangers but that is not always a good idea.

30. I am a source of happiness for many, but I am also a source of sorrow for many. I grow very fast, way fast that most people do not realize when I do. But, I die very slow. Depending on some people and situations, I can be a great pain or great joy.

31. Some call them their Romeo, some call them their world and others call them their superhero. They are very

strong and also very sweet. They buy you gifts, open doors for you, take you out on dates and protect you. Who are they?

32. It has wings, arrows, diapers and is covered in red.

33. You can give it to someone you love. It is very delicate and can easily be broken. It is, however, sweet and pure and given whole.

34. Their goal in life is to save princesses. They are invisible and they eat stars as their favorite delicacy. They are very jumpy and go through the mushroom kingdom. They are said to be originally from Italy.

35. A bit hairy, though very cuddly, it is sweet, sometimes funny, other times annoying and very lovable sometimes. What is it?

36. We are flowers, but not ordinary flowers. We can French kiss and even smooch. What kind of flowers are we?

37. It is a body part that you give wholly to someone you like. However, it can be broken and that aches, throbs and even bleeds without any visible blood. What is it?

18

CHRISTMAS RIDDLES FOR KIDS

1. I appear in various dazzling colors. I shine and twinkle like the stars in the sky. I am used as a decoration because I make houses look so beautiful and feel more like Christmas.
2. It is a very catch Christmas carol that everyone loves to sing along because it has rhyming tunes. It also has 12 different gifts that are given out during the Christmas season. What is it?
3. I am a decoration, but for you to use me, you have to cut me down. I also have wings on one of my sides. What am I?
4. It is something that you wear and is stuffed. It also looks like it could be a giant's socks. What is it?
5. Imagine that a lion was going to release a Christmas music album. What do you think the lion would name the album?
6. What do you think the Christmas tree said to the Christmas stocking?

7. The turkey refused to eat during Christmas. And it was not having a bad stomach. Why did it refuse to eat?

8. Just when Santa was about to go out and hand over all the gifts he had, he got sick and his legs could not move. So he asked to be taken to a hospital where the doctor was going to help him walk comfortably again. The doctor gave him something that would support him as he walked. What did the doctor give to Santa to help him walk?

9. An apple and a Christmas tree got a baby. What did the two name their baby?

10. What did the snowman eat as a snack?

11. The end of the year is 31st December. So what is the end of Christmas?

12. There is a certain type of egg that you can drink, what is it called?

13. What is red and white three times?

14. Assuming you went out in a blizzard and saw a vampire. What do you think you would get?

15. Others keep their money in riverbanks. Where does Frosty the Snowman hide his money?

16. What was it that the doctor told the Christmas bell when they were at the hospital?

17. What happens when you cross a bird and a turtle?

18. What detergent do you think Santa uses for his laundry?

19. What do you think the water globe and the snow globe felt during Christmas season?

20. He is the most impolite and disrespectful of all the Reindeers. Who is he?

21. Why was the chicken allowed to join the boy playing drums at the band?

22. The snowman was feeling itchy and very dry on his head so he went to see the dermatologist for treatment. So,

what does the snowman get when he itches his dandruffs?

23. Where does Santa and his wife Mrs. Claus go for swimming?
24. When people wear me, it means they are celebrating some victory. I am a combination of flowers and leaves and they are put in a circle. Sometimes am very big, but other times, I am very tiny. Who am I?
25. What happens in all the homes after all the Christmas gifts have been opened?
26. What phobia is as a result of seeing Santa Claus?
27. Why is it that Mr. and Mrs. Santa Claus never had a baby Santa?
28. How do children know that Santa Claus had been in the room on Christmas?
29. What happened when Snow woman was angry at Snow man?
30. What do you call a broke and money-less Santa?
31. Why is it that men are so afraid of Christmas?
32. What is an elf dancing with earmuffs called?
33. What is the one part of a snowman that a snow woman cannot resist?
34. What do you think Warren Buffet loves most about Christmas?
35. What is a male angel likely to say to a very beautiful female angel?
36. What is the difference between the English and Christmas alphabets?
37. What are the relatives of Mr. and Mrs. Claus called?
38. What was Mrs. Santa given by Mr. Santa on Christmas for being naughty?
39. The three wise men who went to see baby Jesus travelled by a horse,

elephant and a camel. The Santa rides in a sleigh. What do elves ride on?

40. What did those terrorist groups get for presents on Christmas?

41. Santa had been planning for a long time to buy a new sleigh. However, when he went to buy one, he found that it was free and therefore, did not have to use any money. How was this possible?

42. What is Santa's favorite technological gadget?

43. What type of bug is most likely to hate Christmas?

44. What do elves go to learn at school?

45. What do snow men and snowwomen eat for breakfast?

46. Who gave baby shark their Christmas presents?

47. How did the boys scare away the snowman?

48. What is a snowman called in summer time?

49. What is a child's all time favorite Christmas king?

50. How did the Mexican sheep say Merry Christmas?

51. What would Mr. and Mrs. Claus name their firstborn baby?

52. What Christmas carol do all parents love?

53. What made the Christmas tree refuse to stand up?

54. What is most likely to happen if Santa Claus was deep fried?

55. What would happen if people ate Christmas decorations?

56. Why are all mothers so excited about Christmas?

57. Where does Santa store his costume after Christmas?

58. What makes Santa so good at karate?

59. The reindeer looked at the elf and said something to him. What was it that he said?

60. What is Santa's best cereal for breakfast?

61. What is the name given to Santa when he does not make any movements?

62. What do you think is Santa's nationality?

63. I go inside a chimney red but come out of it black. Who am I?

64. What Music album did the monkeys release on Christmas Eve?

65. Why were all the kids afraid of Santa Claus when Santa came to hand them their presents?

66. I am always green, the bushier I am the more I am loved. All the decorations are seen better when put on me. There's no complete Christmas without me in your homes.

67. It goes around the world and never gets lost. Its work is to help Mr. Santa pull his sleigh. What is it?

68. I am something you eat, but you do not have to cook me first. I look like a hook and the best idea is to lick me instead of biting on me. I come in two colors what am I?

69. It is all stuffed, but no one knows how it is done. However, everyone knows how to use it, is something you wear. What is it?

70. Sometimes Mr. Santa is so busy that he would forget all your gifts and you would have to buy them from the stores. However, since am his helper, I ensure that he packs all your toys that are presented to you on Christmas. Who am I?

71. I am a plant who comes up at Christmas time. People hang me above and like to stand beneath as they kiss. What kind of a plant am I?

72. No one wants strangers breaking into their homes or going in without their permission. However, on Christmas, there is always that one stranger that is welcomed in every house. People do not mind if he breaks into their homes because he is nice and does not destroy or steal anything. He is an old man with very white and long beards. Who is he?

73. They are used as decorations in homes. They can be used anytime, but they look weird if used on any other day other than Christmas. To use them, you need electricity and then they will start sparkling like the stars. What are they?

74. It has a round shape and can be made from evergreens, berries or pine cones. You will not miss it on people's doors during Christmas time. What is it?

75. It has three people that are holding gifts. It also has some animals in it. There are also shepherds, parents, and angels. Then at the center of it all, there is a small baby.

76. Some say I am white, others say am colorless. I drop from the skies and each round, I drop down in a different shape. I think am more beautiful than all the rains. What am I?

77. You can open this every day. You will find something that cannot be beaten. Then behind those doors, you will find something very tasty that is a treat. What is it?

78. Everyone is always hungry during Christmas and always looking forward to trying all the delicacies. But, I am never hungry on this day. Who do you think I am?

79. I am a Santa's reindeer, but you will always spot me on Valentines'. Who am I?

80. It is one of Santa's reindeer that can be seen in the outer space.

81. What did Mr. Adam say to his wife the night before Christmas?

82. Why are all the Christmas trees so bad at knitting?

83. I am the fastest of all the Santa's reindeers.

84. What is the all-time favorite gift that anyone can receive from Santa?

85. On Christmas Eve, Santa is always spotted in his work-
shop, which is in the North Pole. When he leaves the
north, where does he go?

86. There is a time when Christmas and New Year both come
in the same year. When is that?

87. How can you really tell if Santa is a werewolf?

88. What is the best gift you can give a railway station manager for Christmas?

19

WINTER RIDDLES

1. It falls from the skies and lands down as white, tiny stars. They bring a lot of cold, but they are also very fun as you get to play so many fun games. What is it?
2. It helps keep your hands warm when the winter is too deep in. You cannot afford to go out without them on your hands because you will freeze out.
3. Where we live, it is very cold and, therefore, we have to make sure that we are tightly huddled. We have wings, but our wings cannot help us fly. So, we cannot fly to greater heights where it is lesser cold. Who are we?
4. When it has just snowed, you will find it very useful. You just need to take it at the top of a hill. Once there, you can sit on it then slide down the hill.
5. If you want to have fun in the winter season, you need these. They help you play a very popular winter sport. You just need to go on top of a hill, strap these on your feet, then glide down the mountainside with all your friends and you will be having so much fun.
6. Sometimes they make me out of fur, while other times they make me from leather. You can wear me if you want to but you have to be going out where it is very cold.

7. You will see it outside when its winter season and some-times when you are walking around in town. It is caused by frozen water that has dripped down. What is it?

8. Lay down out in the winter air and lay on the white flakes. Make movement with your arms and legs and then get up from that spot? What is it you will leave behind from the spot you were lying on?

9. Winter seasons can be extremely cold. You, therefore, need to keep warm in every area of your body. This item is used to keep your neck warm. What is it?

10. I am evergreen and I come subdivided into branches. You will most likely spot me in the month of December. Who am I?

11. I help keep you warm, especially when it is the winter season. However, if you are not careful with me, I can burn you. Sometimes I go out through the chimney where Santa lands. Who do you think I am?

12. It is something that you make during the winter season. It stands in the form of a human being and all you need to make it is winter flakes, a scarf, a carrot and a coal. Then you have the biggest motionless friend ever. What is it?

13. I was discovered about 1000 years ago by Greek philoso-phers. I am numbered in a straight line and can be used in so many ways. I am especially important during the winter season since I can predict if the rain will turn into snow or not. What am I?

14. If you want us in plenty, you will find us in Greenland. We are in a box and we can be a very great treat. However, there is one place that you will never find us: the oven because it is not a very friendly place for us. What are we?

15. They live in the North Pole and are always heavily dressed up. Their houses are white and they almost survive on one main popular meal called the Paleo. Who are they?

16. Sometimes I am made of flowers while other times I am made of leaves. I am always given a round shape and when people wear me, it is always to celebrate victory. Sometimes I am very big, while other times I am too tiny. What am I?

17. Some think I am a fairy, but sometimes I am too much and can be horrible and spread my ice everywhere. What am I?

18. They are crystals, but when they hit the ground they never break. What kind of crystals are they?

19. What makes negative zero below zero and minus zero all the same?

20. Sometimes, we are made of wool while other times we are made of leather. We come in pairs and always keep you warm when it is the winter season.

21. I am four-sided, tiny and can spin. You can play, but you will have to bet with your chocolate coins if you want to win. What am I?

22. I am made of metal and sometimes plastic. If you want me as metal, then you want me for work, but if you want me as plastic, then you want me for play. I am mostly stored in the sandbox and brought out in the winter because then, I am most useful. What am I?

23. I come unexpected and can be very dreadful. I am sometimes very bitter which makes me very violent. I know you do not like me because I can spoil all your day's plans. Who am I?

24. These three months: January, February and December have something in common. What is it?

25. I am very beautiful just as much as the snow is. However, I am not very cold like the snow is. What am I?

26. It happens only once every four years on snow or ice. When it happens, people do all they can to win and break the title. What is it?

27. I am huge; I destroy and come as a big pile of fluff. I do not walk or run, I just flow and when I do, you better run as fast as you can. What am I?

28. I am a fiery shrub and if you miss me any other time, there is no way you will not see me when it is Christmas season. I look like flowers. Some may think I am, but I am just some green leaves on a tree.

29. It has feathers, but even if it wanted to, it cannot fly. It is very royal, but it does not make it a king. It lays eggs, but is not a chicken. What is it?

30. Sometimes it is found in Canada, other times it is in Alaska and other times in Russia. You will, however, never find it in Africa. What is it?

31. It is fluffy, cold and white. You will often see it in the month of December, but it definitely makes everything look so bright. What could it be?

32. I come in different types and colors. I am something you eat and also something you drink. I am very important because I can help keep you away from the doctor. Who am I?

33. Sometimes I am made from wood, other times plastic and sometimes, I am made of steel. You put me on and I help you slide down the snowy mountains. What am I?

34. You will see me everywhere on the arctic. Huskies help pull me down the mountains. What am I?

35. You can make it very easily. First, you need to make rolls then start molding it. When you are satisfied with the results, you can hang a scarf around it and then put a few

coals or even carrots. You have to make sure it is firm. What is it?

36. It is worn to protect you from the very cold weather in winter. It is made of different materials like fur, wool, plastic and leather. What is it?

37. I stand tall and in very bright green. On Christmas, I am decorated with many bright lights. People like to place their gifts beneath me. You all know who I am.

38. I have the power to make a dark room glow, although I sometimes stand as a sore thumb. I guide others on how to keep the presents flowing. Who am I?

39. It is something that looks like a giant's socks. But we always look forward to it since it has pretty nice surprises inside.

40. If you lit it on Christmas Eve, Santa will not come down from it and you will not get any presents.

41. I am shaped like a ball and, therefore, i am round. However, I cannot bounce, neither can I be dribbled. What am I?

42. Sometimes I am dark and other times white. Sometimes I am cold, while other times I am hot. You want me, but it is better not to have plenty of me. Do you know me?

43. What can appear as caps, sometimes beds and other times as birds?

44. Celsius, Fahrenheit and Kelvin all have one thing in common. What is it?

45. I am celebrated for 8 straight days. During the celebrations, there are very bright lights and very many awesome gifts. I also have potatoes. What am I?

46. Winter is so good to me. It is when I grow and sharpen. Summer, on the other hand, is very unfriendly to me. The warmth kills me instantly. What am I?

47. I like to be warm, but you will only see me in the cold months and always standing outside. I am made of winter flakes. But, you do not know who I am.

48. It is very cold. It has no teeth, but it can bite and does bite. What is it?

49. Sometimes I am all you need for your toes to keep warm during winter. What am I?

50. I am a drink for the young and the old. Some people like to add Marshmallows on me, but either way, I help keep everyone warm when you are feeling cold and shaky. What type am I?

51. When I am born, I do fly. When I am living, I just lie down. But, when I die, I run very fast. What am I?

52. Why were all the angels lying down during winter?

53. What month is the coldest of all the other months of the year?

54. What does Santa use when he wants to go skiing?

55. One polar bear stole icebergs from his fellow polar bears. What is the new name he was given?

56. Why did the skeleton hate the old so much?

57. When did Mr. Snowman ask Mrs. Snowwoman to dance with him?

58. Snowmen have an all-time favorite Mexican dish. Which one do you think it is?

59. What is a very old snowwoman called?

60. What gift did Mrs. Snowwoman buy her husband?

61. What did Snowman ask to be treated for lunch?

62. What is the name you give to a party thrown by snowmen?

63. What type of ball does not bounce?

64. What do turtles do when it is very cold in the winter?

65. What do snowmen like for breakfast?

66. What is the worst thing about snow boots?

67. What is a bird called in the winter season?

68. Why did all the birds fly south for the winter?

69. I am very cold and I do not have a soul. I love the cold; a little warmth will soon kill me. Who am I?

70. I take over every time after fall. When I do, everything will grow, even if slowly. What am I?

71. Why did the snowman name his favorite dog Frost?

72. If you want to travel overseas, then you need to buy a suitcase. If you want to log flames at home, then what do you need?

73. I have snow-white color, I like swimming as much as fish do. I am a very large mammal, but I am not a whale. I am also furry, but no, I am not a dog. You will find me on the North Pole, but I am not Santa. I am very heavy: almost a ton heavy. Who am I?

20

HALLOWEEN RIDDLES

1. It is a very common little bug. However, even though it is so small, most people fear it so much. There is a name for this fear. It is called arachnophobia. Who is this little guy?

2. Imagine you were at a very strange house. Then suddenly, you hear a very weird sound. You cannot see anything, but I can see you since am floating above you. What am I?

3. They lived in the northern and southern areas. Those were the good ones. The bad ones, who were not liked by anyone, came from the eastern and the western areas. They all flew in broomsticks. Who are they?

4. You pump it, but it is not a tire. It is a fluid and a vampire's all-time meal. What is it?

5. They have wings and are very tiny. They are however very scary and only the very brave can go near them and even touch them. You will always find them hanging upside down and mostly in caves. Who are they?

6. It is a body that has no ears and no tongue. He cannot do normal stuff like pick calls or anything else that normal

people do. But this is because he is only made of bones. Who is he?

7. They never come out during the day because the light is harmful to them. If you decide to wait for them at night, they might catch you and bite on your neck. What are they?

8. Archeologists are always very cautious when digging up old tombs. This is because they might run into this monster that is wrapped in linen and may bring them doom. What is this monster?

9. It is a hairy creature and it does not like people. If ever you come across it, you should run very fast. You are only a little safe, if you have a gun that has silver bullets. What is this creature?

10. They are vertebrae and ribs. They are also skulls and phalanges. They are also Femur and sternum. But what are they?

11. It was brought to life by using electricity. It is made up of different body parts with bolts in the neck and skin yellow. What is it?

12. You will find it placed on your front door. You need to remove its seeds and carve a face. What do you think it is?

13. You use it and witches use it too. Witches use it for travel because they can fly around with it, while you use it to keep your room clean. What is it?

14. No one wants to sleep here. When you finally get to lay there, then it means you have left everything you loved behind. Once the lid is closed, that is the end of you, and you are buried for good. What is it?

15. It is a very big black pot used by witches. Inside of it, brews an eye of newt, a toe of a frog, and a wool of a bat. What is its name?

16. It is a popular place, but no one ever wants to be there. Woe unto you if you are stuck there. It is full of many scary ghosts. Where is this place?

17. If you do not want bad luck in your life, then you need to avoid this as much as you can, especially at night. It is a very dark creature that is said to bring bad luck to people. What is it?

18. You will find a hundred of this in the graveyard. But, in this you will not find any dead bodies. You will, however, find all the information about all the dead bodies in each burial place.

19. All ghosts dread to be in this room. They would rather be anywhere else but in this one room. Which is it?

20. How do you spell Candy in just two letters?

21. Ghosts have a favorite spot on the road that they always want to travel at. Which is it?

22. Black cats are said to be bad luck. But, when is the one time you are guaranteed of bad luck when you cross the black cat?

23. Snap, Pop and crackle were all very scared. What happened?

24. Why did the mummy never make any friends?

25. What did the ghost order as a desert when he went to the restaurant?

26. Why did the monster eat everyone else, but not the crazy person?

27. Where do were wolfs like to hide?

28. What is the best way to fix a jack-o-lantern?

29. What is the ghost's favorite makeup?

30. What did the terrible spider say to the poor fly on Halloween?

31. Why did the vampire enroll in the art school?

32. You and a ghost are in the same room. But when you look around you are the only one. How is this possible?

33. Where are baby ghosts left when their parents go to work?

34. What do you get when you cross a snowman and a witch?

35. There was once a very popular skeleton who was a detective. What was his name?

36. What instrument did the skeleton play?

37. What were the ghost's favorite fruits?

38. What was the favorite thing for ghosts to do on Saturday night?

39. What do witches ask for when they stop at a hotel?

40. What would you say if you met a ghost in your bedroom?

41. What is the name given to ghosts who are out of work?

42. What made the game warden arrest the ghost?

43. When is the only time when witches stop on the highway?

44. Why would witches buy magazines?

45. What do goblins sing in the shower?

46. I am a body; I have a head, arms and head. However, I always look naked. Guess who I am.

47. I am packaged, but I am not a gift. I have an archeologist's best treasure and I am kept in chambers. Who am I?

48. It is rectangular and hollow and has a lid. It is buried six feet underground. What is it?

49. What is the name given to a funny skeleton that makes you giggle and laugh?

50. Some people believe I exist, but others do not believe. Those that do, believe that I come out at night and that I either float or roam around looking for people to scare. What am I?

51. I hate the rain and people hate me just as much because they believe that I am bad luck. What am I?

52. Where do ghosts, mummies and zombies love to go swimming?

53. It is small, scary and goes around zipping at night. What is it?

54. A Dracula will draw and bank this item. What is it?

55. It is dead, cold and hard and surrounds the cemetery.

56. What happens when you cross a teacher and a Dracula?

57. It is homeless, but no one will take it in because it is very wicked. It is white and will always go up and down.

58. Where do mummies and zombies go when they are very exhausted from working?

59. The witch has a broomstick; the jack o'lantern has a candle. So what does a vampire have?

60. It comes in Orange, it is very hollow and very smart. What is it?

61. What is very red, juicy, delicious, and could be equally poisonous, if it was given to you by the wicked woman?

62. He is very old, has a long white beard, and gives out the best presents. But, on Halloween day we all forget him. Who is he?

63. I am found in the quietest, yet very creepy place. For people to come in, they have to die first. What am I?

64. What are you likely to get when you cross some alcohol and lightning bug?

65. He is a very powerful man. He looks like a pumpkin although he is always dressed in black. His name is written all over, even in the most popular buildings. Who is he?

66. Are you good at math? If so, what is the ratio of a Jack O'lantern's circumference to its diameter?

67. How do you tell which witch is the witch?

68. It is very heavy, almost 5000lbs. It is gray and has the longest nose ever and flies on a broom. What is it?

69. Mirror, mirror please do tell. Who is the ugliest of them all?

70. It can be sour and sweet and can also be hard and soft all at once. What is it?

71. Who is always the hottest person at all the Halloween parties?

72. If peanut butter has jelly, Bonnie has Clyde, and a pea has a pod, what will a skeleton have?

73. Where do all the ghosts and all the spirits drop off their parcels and letters?

74. Zombies, Mummies, Vampires and witches all have one thing in common. What is it?

75. They are small, brown, blind, very creepy, and only come out at night. They like dark places. What are they?

76. Ghosts and vampires look for me when it is very dark on an autumn night. They come with a ding and a buzz, waiting with open arms for me. What am I?

77. He is very huge, has a big scar on his head, green, and likes to trick and scare away all the children when it is Halloween day. Who is he?

78. When you celebrate me, there are a lot of pranks, pumpkins and you get a lot of treats. I am the only holiday you get to enjoy best when it is dark. Some think am a scary day while others can wait to try new outfits on this day. What am I?

79. Which would be the best day to carve out Jack O'lantern?

80. Sometimes I am yellow, sometimes pink, while other times I am red. But, most times I am green. I am delicious, but one time I was used in the wrong way. An evil woman once used me to poison someone. I am not evil though, I help you not have many doctor visits. Who am I?

81. Every once a year, I am the attention of every household. On this day, people can use me for a pie, but will mostly use me by decorating me in various styles.

21

SHORT RIDDLES

1. What is the type of goose that fights with snakes?
2. I get wet when am drying. What am I?
3. People cannot stay without answering me yet I never ask them any questions.
4. I am a word, a simple word, but most people always pronounce me wrong. Who am I?
5. Its fruit is on the leaves and the leaves are on the fruit. What is it?
6. It can be in any shape, but it can be small and sometimes big. When you have it, you do not keep it.
7. It has one eye but cannot see.
8. There is a girl outside a store. She cannot read the signs at the store but she is aware she needs to go in and buy something. Which store is she at?
9. A man was riding to town on his horse. He went to town on Monday, stayed there for some days and came back on Friday. How did that happen when he was not even feeling exhausted?
10. Tuesday, Ben and Jim went to a restaurant where they were to give themselves treats. They ate all the favorite

meals, paid the bill and left. However neither Ben nor Jim paid the bill. Who paid it for them?

11. It stinks; it comes from one hole and goes right into two other holes.

12. What is the common thing between a very dirty rug and a bad boy?

13. It is something very precious. Once you lose it, it can never be returned
to you.

14. You have 5 apples and there are 6 people. They all want an apple. How do you divide it among them?

15. No matter where you go, you will use me. I am always flat and you need me every day. I am the reason you wake up very early in the morning every day. But, you give me away all the time. I am colored and have a founding father on me.

16. This something is always full during the day, but when it is nighttime, it is empty. What is it?

17. It is very slippery and greasy. It is very calm when inside, but once it gets out, it cannot keep calm and keeps jumping up and down. What is it?

18. It has the power to cut the wind. It is a blade, it is slim, and very sharp. What is it?

19. Which is the noblest instrument of them all?

20. Some chins are never shaved. Which are they?

21. I am the highest mark in the class. I appear in two most common places: In the laptop and in a human's t-shirt. Usually when people describe me, I am described as something above. What am I?

22. It is an instrument that plays from the heart.

23. Someone who is in jail and a sinking ship have something in common.

24. No one can enter this place, no matter who they are. Everyone would want to visit here, but you cannot really get there in life. Where is this place?

25. I am just like a dog. I have a tail and it wags just like a dog's, but am not a dog. Who am I?

26. I am needed for survival. If you want to be happy, you need me, but I bring both good and evil. You can use me and still get another me. You have to seek me to find me. When am gone, you can always find others like me.

27. For bird, it means freedom, but for old men, it means they can write comfortably. What is it?

28. When is a bright idea similar to a clock?

29. Everyone has them, but Adam and Eve never had them. What are they?

30. Why were tennis players arrested?

31. Bob was at a movie theatre when he jumped and fell over 30 feet. However, he did not get any injury, and neither was he scratched. How did that happen?

32. There were 10 birds resting on a branch. Then a man who was passing by came and shot at 5 of the birds. How many were left?

33. What is a show that prisoners are most likely to put on?

34. Who was the most popular cat in the wild west?

35. Why does the light shine?

36. It is dressed when night falls and undressed when it is daybreak.

37. My mother holds me and keeps me safe. But, before I die, I kiss her.

38. I can fool you, especially when you have no idea what you are doing. You can see me day and night. What am I ?

39. An American guy died and went to hell. What do you think he said once there?

40. I am something that every young woman desires. Once they have me, they are bound for life. I make them so happy.
41. It has teeth, but does not use its teeth for chewing food. What is it?
42. Trees in the winter and troublesome visitors have it in time. What do they do?
43. What is a pirate's favorite word?
44. I am blind during the day, but when it is nighttime, I see very clearly. Who am I?
45. A father has 9 children and half of them are girls. How is this possible?
46. When does a human being become like a snake?
47. What type of money are vampires most likely to use?
48. What animal is most likely to like doors?
49. If a man is struggling to get his appetite back, what is the one country he should visit?
50. It is the biggest room in the whole world. What room is this?
51. Every time you see her, she will always be pregnant. But, she never gives birth to a young one. Who is she?
52. You are always going to find me during meal times. But, there is one time of the day that you will never find me: nighttime. Who am I?
53. What is just made of two hands, a longer hand, and a shorter hand?
54. What is a five-letter word that becomes smaller once you put two more letters to it?
55. It has a neck, but does not have a head. What is it?
56. What made the little boy burry his flashlight?
57. It is the only letter in the alphabet that has the most water. Which is it?

58. It is a word that has a thousand letters. It starts with P and ends with E. What is it?
59. It is only useful to you when it is broken. What is it?
60. Why would a person living in California not be buried in New York?
61. It starts with a T, has a T in it, and ends with a T. What is it?
62. Which month of the year has 28 days?
63. Four men were sailing on a boat when it capsized. Only three got their hair wet. What happened to the fourth man?
64. How many letters does the Alphabet have?
65. When does Friday come before Thursday?
66. There is a ship that has two mates but, does not have a captain. Which is it?
67. Ann's mother has five daughters. Tata, Tetu, Titi, Totu. What is the name of the fifth daughter?
68. It occurs once in a million, twice in a millimeter, and not once in a hundred years. What is it?
69. It is the most delicate thing ever. Even by just saying its name, you have already broken it. What is it?
70. There is a certain type of tree that anyone carries around easily and effortlessly. Which is it?
71. If an electric train is going north, what will be the direction of the smoke from the train?
72. They are never stolen, but can never be seen during the day. They will come out at night, even when no one has called them. Who are they?
73. Why do the lions and all other wild animals eat raw meat?
74. It keeps going up, but never comes down. No one has control over it.
75. What would be the last thing you take off before going to bed?

76. What would happen if you went swimming at the Red Sea with a white costume?

77. It has a total of four legs, but you will never see it walking.

78. How would you make the number one disappear?

79. There is a monkey, a bird and a squirrel. They decide to race up on the top of a coconut tree and whoever gets there first would get the banana. Who do you think got the banana?

80. What has letter T and an island have in common?

81. What three days do not mention any of the seven days of the week?

82. What would you call a fairy who never takes a bath?

83. Which word is spelled incorrectly?

84. Why are teddy bears never hungry at all?

85. What name would be given to a funny book about eggs?

86. What would you do if you had stubborn dandruffs? What would you use as a cure?

87. Why would a man not have all his fingers on one hand?

88. What did the beach say when the tide came?

89. Which football player would wear the biggest helmet?

90. What did the outlaw gain after stealing the calendar?

91. How do rabbits travel when they want to go on vacations?

92. What bank is ever broke with no money?

93. It has so many rings but, does not have fingers.

94. What are the two things that you can never ever have for dinner?

95. What type of cup can you never drink on?

96. Why did the bumble bee put honey under his pillow?

97. Which is the longest word ever?

98. Which weighs more, a gram of salt or a gram of wheat?

99. If four friends namely green, yellow, blue and orange all lived in houses called just like their names, who would live in the white house?

100. It goes through almost everywhere. It goes through all towns, hills and even villages. But, it never makes a single movement. What is it?

101. You can look back on memories, but you can never see this again.

102. Two is company and three is a crowd. What are four and five?

103. What is the center of gravity?

104. A hat maker, a plumber, and a lawyer were walking together. Which one had the biggest hat?

105. Which room has no rooms or doors?

106. Who is the fastest runner that ever existed?

107. You have it and is rightfully yours. However, everyone else uses it more than you.

108. It has so many holes but can still hold so much water.

109. What stones are never found in the ocean?

110. I have no locks, but I have so many keys. You can enter, but can never go outside.

111. Four men went out camping and each carried their own tent. However, only three people actually carried the tents. Why did this happen?

112. In the morning I have 4 legs. Later in the day, I walk with my 2 feet, and then, very late before dark, I have 3 legs. What am I?

113. It is something that everyone has. It is very light, but no one can hold it for more than a minute.

114. What word when pronounced right, is wrong and when pronounced wrong, it is right?

115. I cannot talk and cannot hear as well. But, I always tell the truth.

116. It goes around villages, towns, cities, and most of other places, but never goes inside.
117. What has no legs, but is always running?
118. What dies, but does not have a life?
119. It has cities, but no humans live in it: it has rivers but there is no water in it: it has forests, but there are no trees and animals.
120. It always gets answered, even though it never asks any questions.
121. Unlike others who are born small and get big as they grow, I was born big and get smaller as I grow.
122. It is always coming but never arrives.
123. I have so many keys, but I can never open a door.
124. It is what you get after a colorful rainbow.
125. Only poor people have me, rich people do not have me. If you rely on me you die.
126. Almost everyone wants water for survival. For me, however, water is my worst enemy. What am I?
127. You make me happen, yet the more you take me further, the more you leave me behind.
128. Everyone buys it with the intention of eating, but no one ever eats it.
129. The one who makes it does not make it for himself. The one who buys it does not buy it for himself and the one who uses it is not aware they are using it.
130. When it rains, water comes down and it goes up. What is it?
131. You cannot see me and you do not even have to touch me, but you make me and break me.
132. As a baby, it is very tall, but when old it becomes very short.
133. It has no legs and has no bones, but when you keep it warm, it can walk away after some time.

134. If it eats it survives, if it drinks it dies.
135. Without the head, it is high, but with the head, it goes lower.
136. You remove my clothes and cook the inner me. Then you eat the outer me and throw the inner me.
137. It is something that has been there for so many years but has never grown beyond one month.
138. It is born in the air and speaks, although it does not have a mouth.
139. It grows the more you take away from it.
140. To have it, you must never share it. If you share it, you lose it.
141. Once you catch it you want to throw it away, but you cannot. What is it?
142. You beat it and whip, but you never see it crying.
143. Once it comes down, it can never get back up.
144. It has so many limbs, but does not have the power to walk.
145. It is a dress that can never be worn.
146. You may be a lucky person, but you can never win this bet.
147. It hangs and flies around all day, but never leaves the spot.
148. It goes up and down, but never moves. What is it?
149. It has a bark, but it cannot bite.
150. Getting into it is so easy, but getting out of it is very hard.
151. It has a neck and wears a cap, but does not have a head.
152. What is the one thing that a cat has that no other animal has?
153. What does not remove its shoes before going to sleep?
154. What is big like an elephant, but has not weight at all?
155. What fur do you get from a tiger?
156. What has a horn but never honks at all?

157. What two popular keys cannot open doors?

22

WHO AM I RIDDLES

1. I am my father's child and also my mother's child. But, I am no one's son, who am I?
2. I will be there Tomorrow, I was there Yesterday, but I am nowhere to be seen Today.
3. I am a 5-letter word. When you take away the first letter, I become the name of a place. When you take the first two letters, I then become the opposite of the original word. Who am I?
4. My work is to save lives especially on water. My first four letters represent all the living things. The last five letters also mean a guard. Who am I?
5. My work is hard and sometimes easy. I get to craft crowns of silver and gold. Who am I?
6. My home is in the sky. People say am hot and bright and so you are not supposed to look at me directly. You will never see me when it is nighttime. Who am I?
7. I am delicate and can easily be broken. I am the symbol of love and I live inside you. Who am I?
8. I am round and go up and down. I am the reason why most boys get into trouble. You can easily throw and catch me. Who am I?

9. Everyone loves to pick me up. Sometimes, I like it and sometimes, I do not. I like smiling, but most times, you will find me crying. My favorite meal and snack is milk. Who am I?

10. Kids love to climb me. Birds make me their home. I love the rains because then, I can live for so many years. I am green, but sometimes I am brown. Who am I?

11. I have very many colors and smell really nice. If you want me, you can just pick me up or buy me. If you want me to live with you longer, you have to give me enough water. Who am I?

12. If I get big when full and if you do not hold me down or tie me, I will float. When you break me, I will make the loudest noise ever. Who am I?

13. I can attach to your wall and I look like a cube. I entertain you and most people cannot keep off me.

14. I am always in pairs and you need to tie and untie me. I give you comfort, but when am wet, I can make you very uncomfortable.

15. I have a button, a zipper, pockets and sometimes I come with a belt. You cannot do without me on winter, but on summer, you can put me aside.

16. I am a treat and kids will do anything to have me. You can only have me when it is hot. I come either in a bowl or in a cone.

17. I am a ball that you can roll, but you can never bounce me up and down.

18. I have a horn and I can give you milk, but I am not an animal. Who am I?

19. You will only hear and even see me mostly at night. I have four legs, but have no tail. Who am I?

20. I love cleaning so much, but every time I clean, I become smaller and smaller. What am I?

21. I have all the five fingers that a human has. But, am not the hand and neither am I alive. What am I?

22. I do not have wings, but I sure can fly. I cry sometimes, but I do not have eyes. Do you know me?

23. When I walk, I jump. When I stand, I sit. Who am I?

24. I do not have arms or legs, but I do have a head and a tail.

25. You like me; I look like a Nut inside a hole.

26. When you point me up, I will make everything bright. When you point me down, nothing else can be seen.

27. It is a fruit, but it is different from other fruits because its seeds are on the outside. What am I?

28. If you want to wake up early in the morning, you can count on me. I do not need electricity or batteries, but I will definitely wake you up. Who am I?

29. I have two eyes like most creatures and they are on my face. However, I have other many eyes that are on my tail.

30. I am a big party and you celebrate me at night. But, I will always give you a big fright every once in a year.

31. It is the very treat you can have on summer. It is pink and you cannot resist eating it.

32. People call me old school, but I do not think I am useless. You can still visit me because I am always open. However, you left me for the internet and now I am always lonely and feeling empty. Who am I?

33. I am what you need to begin all your sentences. What am I?

34. It is a shiny soft metal that you use to cover your food. What is it?

35. You must get to me first and touch me if you want to reach to second. What am I?

36. If you are lucky enough, sometimes you will catch me as I hop in your homes hiding eggs. Who am I?

37. People say that black scares them, but I am white and I will surely scare you. Who am I?

38. When people are done using their boats, I will help keep the boats safe in water and will not allow the boats to be swayed away by water.

39. I am sweet when undressed, but my clothes can cause very terrible falls if you leave them on the ground. Monkeys are my biggest fans. What am I?

40. Grandmas and aunts love me the most because they get to pinch on me.

41. For you to see me, you have to be really nice all year long. Who am I?

42. If you are a bird or any other creatures with feathers you will want to make me your home. What am I?

43. Most people own me, but the most popular of them all is old McDonald. What am I?

44. I am usually small, I live in the middle of the water, but I am a land. What am I?

45. I have every color you know, but there is no gold in me. What am I?

46. I am the only type of fish that you will find chasing after a mouse. What am I?

47. When you say me, I sound like a parrot. I am orange in color. What am I?

48. I am a dog and every time I see something red I have to chase after it. What am I?

49. If you remove my clothes, I will be embarrassed and I will make you pay for it by making you cry.

50. It has wings and that means it can fly. It can even soar high up in the sky . What am I?

51. I am very tall, but I cannot touch the sky. I like to sway around, but I cannot walk or change positions.

52. It comes in very many different shapes and forms. It will follow you everywhere you go at night and you cannot hide from it if you are outside.
What is it?

53. We are millions and millions of us. You cannot count us even if you try. We shine and make your night outside very beautiful. What are we?

54. I am very safe to use for travel, but most people fear me so much. I will take you around the world if you want me to. What am I?

55. I am a game that all kids love to play, but they can only play m outside. If you are not too careful I will fly far away from you and you will not find me soon. What am I?

56. I can connect you with anyone you want to reach, anywhere in the world. However, most times you are always ignoring me. I am an addiction to so many people and they protect me like a baby. What am I?

57. What is circular from one end to the other, but very high in the middle?

58. Just one time in the morning, then boom! I am two, but zero in the evening.

59. When on some people, I am called curly. On others, I am called bald. Sometimes I am black and sometimes I am gray. I can be very long, but some people keep me short. What am I?

60. The more I grow, the less you see. What am I?

61. You need discipline to maintain me. Even saying my name is enough for me to disappear. What am I?

62. You cannot burn it on fire and neither can you drown it on water. What is it?

63. If you want me to get sharp, you have to keep using me. What am I?

64. I live in the dark but you can always get me when you need to use me. I have eyes but I cannot see. What am I?

65. Once you open me, you cannot close or repair me back no matter how hard you try. What am I

66. If you want to keep away from trouble, you have to follow my instructions. I have three eyes and one leg. What am I?

67. Everyone needs it, but they are always giving it away. What is it?

68. I have no feathers, but I can fly. When you are awake, I am asleep. When you are asleep, I am awake. What am I?

69. You murder me every day, yet every time you can help mourning for me.

70. When you are having me, I am very real. Especially when you are sleeping. When you are awake, is top being real. What am I?

71. I am in every building. I protect you from cold sometimes, but used for light most times. If you touch me too much I get dirty and when you hold me too tight, I will break down. What am I?

72. I can be very sweet, but sometimes I can be very sour. I am called like one of the colors of the rainbow. What am I?

73. If you want to see the insides of a human being, you will use me. What am I?

74. When you do not have me, then you will lose your head. What am I?

75. I am something that everyone needs and my days are numbered. What am I?

76. I do not need any space, but I will always fill up a room. What am I?

77. When you use me, I can go up or I can go down, but I never move. Who am I?

78. I can point out in every direction, but I cannot go to the destination I pointed out by myself. What am I?

79. I have so many legs, but I cannot stand on my own. When I get dirty, then everything else becomes clean. What am I?

80. Try chasing after me, but I can bet you will never catch me.

81. You can make me, you can play me, and even crack me. What am I?

82. I am dry, but when I get in I come out wet. The longer I stay in, the more colorful and shorter I become. What am I?

83. I am a word and very unique because you will still spell me the same way, even when I am spelt upside down. What am I?

23

FUNNY RIDDLES

1. Of all the letters in the alphabet, I am the biggest because I hold the most water.
2. What comes at the end of a rainbow?
3. There was once a woman who was addicted to the color Pink. She lived in a small one-story house and everything was pink. The seats, the walls, and everything in it was pink. What was the color of the stairs?
4. A woman bought 5 apples, went to the house washed them and put them in the fruit rack. She later took 2 apples. So, how many apples did the woman have in total?
5. How do you say Racecar backwards?
6. How is it possible that you tossed a ball very far away from you, but it tossed back at you?
7. What is an odd number, but when you remove one from it, it becomes an even number?
8. A boy was climbing up a 30 feet ladder when he fell down. However, he was not hurt. How is this possible?
9. What would be the meaning of iRIGHT?
10. Imagine you are being chased by a tiger. There is nowhere for you to hide, but there is a tree close by. What would you do?

11. You have a fridge and an elephant you want to put inside the fridge. How would you do this?

12. You have a fridge and you want to let a giraffe in. How would you do this?

13. One day, the king of the jungle called a meeting for all the wild animals. They were going to have a very serious meeting. All the animals attended, but one did not. Which animal never attended the meeting?

14. You have to cross a river that has so many dangerous crocodiles. What would you do?

15. What would be the easiest and fastest way for you to double your money?

16. Everyone has it and no one can steal from another. You can also not lose it you will always have it.

17. There's going to be a reward for anyone who can tell what can be found between earth and heaven. Are you smart enough?

18. Everyone will break me every time they speak. What am I?

19. Why is it that every time you are looking for something lost, you always find it in the last place you look?

20. How can a human being survive for 10 days without sleep?

21. You are in a race of 20 people. You then pass the person who was in the second place. What will be you new position?

22. Why are dragons always asleep during the day?

23. It has no hands, but it can slap you hard. What is it?

24. What is a Frog's favorite sport?

25. What does an insect like to play?

26. What can you find in the middle of March and April, but you can never find in the beginning or at the end of any month?

27. What is always ahead, but you can never touch it or see it?

28. When does Friday come before Thursday?

29. It has 81 teeth, but never brushes what is it?

30. What is usually blue, but will always smell like white paint?

31. What word in the dictionary has three letters that are progressive?

32. What kind of tea do soccer players drink?

33. What can run, but can never walk?

34. When you want to use me, you have to throw me. But, when you have no use for me, you have to store me. What am I?

35. Why did Cyclops stop teaching?

36. A king, a queen and two twins were all lying in one room, but there were no adults in the room. How is this possible?

37. Every time you stand up, you will lose me. What am I?

38. What would happen to frogs if they parked in the wrong place?

39. How does the sky settle its bills?

40. Which is the common building in the world that has so many stories?

41. Why was the old woman seated in her rocking chair while wearing her rollerblades?

42. What do you call a cow that twitches?

43. What is the name given to a dog who is a detective?

44. What do you call an alligator that wears a vest?

45. What did the baseball glove say to the baseball?

46. What is the one thing that you can hold in your right hand, but you can never hold in your left hand?

47. When I am going forward, I am heavy. But, when I am moving back, I am not.

48. What gets wet and wet whenever it dries?

49. What word would still sound the same, even with four of its letters removed?

50. You are fast asleep on your sofa when you are awoken by a burglar who is trying to break into your house. You have a sword safely locked in a safe. What do you open first?

51. It's 2 am and you were going to sleep before some of your friends stepped in to visit you. They are hungry and the only food you have is a pizza, apples and a bag of crackers. What would you open first?

52. An Uber driver was headed downtown when he came across a sign that read "No left-hand turn." He ignored the sign and went on, but he came across some cops who did not arrest him. Why was he not arrested?

53. What was the number of animals that Moses took into the ark?

54. What did the Christmas tree say to the light bulb?

55. Where in the world should you never take a dog?

56. What would you call a cow when there is an earthquake?

57. What is the one thing that is readable and supplied everywhere in the world every morning?

58. Mr. and Mrs. Cow went on a vacation. Where did they stay?

59. If snakes went to school what would be their favorite subjects?

60. Which country in the world are you likely to be more slippery?

61. What happens when an orange takes a test?

62. I grow very tall earlier in the day. When it's mid-day, I become short and later, I am even shorter. I will disappear at night, but you are sure to catch me the next morning. What am I?

63. Why did the big turkey cross the road?

64. Why was the baker arrested?

65. Why does a giraffe have a very long neck?

66. Who has two eyes, but cannot see?

67. What did the cannibal say after he was done eating the clown?

68. What has four eyes, but cannot see?

69. Why did the mummy not answer the ringing phone?

70. Why did the skeleton refuse to cross the road?

71. How do vampires go around?

72. What would be a mummy's favorite song to dance to?

73. Why have skeletons been in existence for so long, yet there is not a single one of them who is famous?

74. What did the little tree say on Halloween?

75. Where did the ghost go to buy his stamps?

76. What kind of roads do young ghosts go to when they want to hunt?

77. Why are the white cats such great singers?

78. What did the witch's son ask for Christmas?

79. How do ugly witches tell time?

80. What did the boy skeleton tell his brother after he was told a lie?

81. Where does that ghost go for swimming?

82. When do ghosts like to cook their meals?

83. What did the full moon vampire say to the other full moon vampire?

84. What do you call ghosts who are roommates?

85. Why was the ghost so lonely at the Halloween party?

86. What did the baby bat say to his mum when he was tucked to sleep?

87. Why do vampires wear name tags?

88. People call me dirty, but they cannot keep away from me. Once in a while, they have to visit me several times a day. What am I?

89. What word in the dictionary is hilarious?

90. How did all the planets manage to form the solar system?

91. I always go out but never in. I am hot, sometimes I am soft and sometimes I am hard. Sometimes, I am runny while other times I am loose. I float sometimes, but most times I sink. What am I?

92. It is a book that most people like both young and old. What is it?

93. What did the three little pigs say as they were running away from the bad wolf?

94. What did the stressed math book say to the calculator, the notebook, and the dictionary?

95. How many seconds are there in February?

96. What did the left eye say to the right eye?

97. What is the best table for all human beings to eat?

98. What is the difference between electricity and lightning?

99. What does not have a body and does not have a nose as well?

100. What part of London can you find in France?

101. What three-letter word will still remain the same, even after removing two letters?

102. What is the color of Kenny's black dog?

103. What is as big as you, but cannot weigh as much as you do?

104. What did one ocean say to the other ocean when they met?

105. What would a leopard do if they wanted to change their spots?

106. When is the one time when you stop at green and move at red?

107. If I fall from a building, I will not die and neither will I be hurt. However, if I touch water, I am surely doomed. What am I?

24

MATH RIDDLES

1. 1 grandfather, fathers and sons all went out to buy burgers. They each ordered a burger. How many burgers did they end up paying for?
2. A man went to a market where he bought a very healthy rooster which he was going to use to lay eggs. He expected the rooster to lay 2 eggs every evening. How many eggs would he have after 2 weeks?
3. A boy was sent out in the market to buy eggs. He bought 20 eggs, but while on his way back, he broke all but 7 of the eggs. How many eggs did he take home?
4. It took 20 men 10 days to build a house. How long would 30 men take to build the same house?
5. What number remains the same no matter what number you multiply it with?
6. How was the soccer fan able to predict that the scores will be 0-0 even before the game began?
7. How is it possible that you can add 9 to 5 and get 2 and still the answer is correct?
8. When you add the son's age to the father's age, the total is 66. When you reverse the son's age, you will get the father's age. How old are the two?

9. A boy has more than two dogs. All the dogs are corgis, but two. All are pugs, but two, and all are labs except two. What types of dogs does the boy have and how many are they?

10. When Ann was 10 years old, her little sister was half her age. If Ann is 30 right now, how old is her sister?

11. What would you put between 5 and 6 to make the result greater than 5, but lesser than 6?

12. The total cost of a notebook and a pen is $140. The notebook cost $ 100 more than the pen. How much is the cost of the pen?

13. What do you think is the furthest a cat can run into the forest?

14. How many times do you have to subtract 5 from 25?

15. What did the math book say to the other math book?

16. One is to three as three is to five and five is to four. Four is the magical number. Explain this puzzle.

17. How can you add 8 to itself to make a total of 1000?

18. What grade did the little lobster attain in his math test?

19. Why is it that counting cows is much easier than counting sheep?

20. What do mathematics teachers like as treats?

21. What happened to the flower that was in the math class?

22. What is the most useful tool that a math teacher will need in their classroom?

23. What do you call two male math best friends?

25

TRICKY RIDDLES

1. What do sea monsters order for when they go to restaurants?
2. What name would be given to a kitten who drinks lemonade?
3. Why was the clock in the cafeteria always running slow?
4. Why was the banana advised to see the doctor?
5. Why did the bicycle refuse to stand on its own?
6. What would you name a song about cars?
7. What did the cookie do to the doctor for?
8. Why was the cake's favorite sport baseball?
9. What type of monkeys can fly around?
10. What did the banana do when he heard an ice scream?
11. What would you do to make a wood box lighter?
12. What is the difference between a jailer and a jeweler?
13. It grows down as it grows up.
14. What will happen when you put a very bright yellow dress inside the red sea?
15. Why do sharks always swim in salty water?
16. Why are all the wild animals in Africa not funs of sports?
17. What is the name given to a zipper on a banana?
18. What do all the lazy dogs do for fun?

19. Wednesday, Susan and Fred went to watch a movie and they bought popcorns. The total bill was $ 15, which they decided to divide amongst themselves. Susan paid $ 5 and Fred paid $5, but who paid for the other $ 5?

20. I may look clean and new sometimes but I am very dirty. People like me and will keep me regardless of how dirty I am. They do not clean me, but they sure make me and change me from time to time. What am I?

21. An old man died in 1990 while he had been born in 1964. However, died at the age of 59

22. Scientists discovered that river Amazon is the longest river in the entire world. Which one was before this discovery?

23. I am every woman's dream. People say that I am the greatest treasure in the whole universe. I am a bit tall and am also a bit wide.

24. There was once a very popular scientist who hated clowns. He was planning on removing 4 heads from a 5 headed man and sow it to the clown he came across. He estimated that removing every head would take 30 minutes per head. What was the overall estimated time for the whole procedure?

25. Scott and Kurtis are great friends. Scott is a smoker while Kurtis is not a smoker. Scott decides to smoke an E-cigarette and Kurtis cannot stand all the smoke from Scott. What can he do to avoid all the smoke?

26. What is word is full of 't' begins with 't' and ends with 't'?

27. Which two siblings are on the opposite side of the road, but they never see each other?

28. What do you do to make a line longer without even touching it?

29. How can a pocket have something in it even though it is empty?

30. I am a three in one. I am a fruit, a bird and a person. What am I?

31. Feed me any time, I will always warm up. However, wet me a little and I vanish.

32. I love flying and I will fly all day long. However, I do not have feathers and neither am I a fly?

33. What loses its head every night and gets it right back every morning?

34. What are the letters you will never miss in every single day of the week?

35. What comes down, but never goes back up?

36. I have so many limbs, but no matter how I try I cannot walk. What am I?

37. Four people can repair four cars in 4 hours. How many cars will 8 people repair in 8 hours?

38. If somebody said tomorrow, that the day before yesterday was Saturday, what day would be today?

39. A shepherd was herding his 20 sheep when all but 12 got lost. How many sheep was the shepherd left with?

40. Which is heavier? One kilogram of salt or one kilogram of rice?

41. What has four legs, but has just one foot?

42. Every single day you have to break this time of the day. Which is it?

43. You can never eat me, but you sure can serve me. What am I?

44. What is ever late, but never in the present?

45. Two monkeys are playing on a tree. One suddenly jumps down and the second one soon jumps down as well. Why did the second monkey jump down?

46. You are walking down the street when you bump into a man. You can see him, but he cannot see you. Why can't he see you?

47. Why was 6 so afraid of 7?

48. What has one eye, but the eye cannot help it see?

49. What is over your head, but under your hat?

50. I have feet, but I cannot walk. I have a nose, but cannot breath. I am very sleepy and I never wake up. Who am I?

51. I am a driver, but no one will ever arrest me no matter how many rules I break. What kind of a driver am I?

52. What states are the most favorite ones for a primary school science teacher?

53. What has three feet, but cannot walk no matter how much they try?

54. You have an empty school bag. How many books would you put in the empty school bag?

55. What goes through every door, but never comes in or goes out?

56. What carried their mad babies?

57. There's nothing I cannot double. Give me a man and I will double him as well. What am I?

58. Everything gets finished when you take something from it. I am different because no matter what you take, I will not stop growing.

59. I have two hands, but when I want to scratch myself i cannot. What am I?

60. When it rains, everything goes down, but I stay up to fight the rains.

61. I do not have wings and neither do I have hands. However, you will always catch me climbing the sky. What am I?

62. If you have me, I am hard to keep. If you share me, then am gone. What am I?

63. What time do all tennis players wake up?

64. What do you have that is moving from left to right, right now

65. Which of all Santa's Claus reindeer's can be seen on Valentine?

66. It has a thousand needles, but you will never find it sewing.

67. A man was in a car when he saw a golden door, a silver door and a bronze door. What door did he open first?

68. I run all around the pasture, but never move. What am I?

69. There are 5 children in a car. Jack and John are twins, but fight a lot so they cannot sit together. Rinda and Linda also fight a lot so they cannot sit together. Max likes fighting his sisters so he can only sit by his brothers. There are 5 seats that are side by side and you have to arrange the kids so that none of them ends up fighting. How do you do this?

70. How many sides does a circle have?

71. I do not ask any questions, but I need so many answers. What am I?

72. What kind of a goose fights with snakes?

73. What runs in towns all day and all night?

74. What is at the end of everything?

75. It has wheels and flies, but it is not an aircraft. What is it?

76. What makes Peter Pan keep on flying?

77. A man who works as a clerk at butchery has a wife and two kids. He is 6 feet 2 tall and his shoe size is 14. What is he likely to weigh?

78. What made the English teacher wear sunglasses when she was teaching?

79. I will always pass before the sun, but I will never make a shadow. What am I?

80. What is the only question that you can never answer with a Yes?

81. How would monkeys make toast?

82. It does not matter how smart you are. You will always overlook this thing, what is it?

83. Why did the little boy bring a ladder to school?

84. It is bigger than you, but you are definitely heavier than it is. What is it?

85. A boy was climbing a 100 foot ladder when he fell down. However, he was not hurt. How was he not hurt?

86. The more it is, the less you see. What is this?

87. If you went to space, what kind of music would you listen to?

88. Sometimes I am born silently, while other times I will just be too loud. You cannot see me, but you will definitely feel my presence. After some time, I will disappear without a trace. I am not harmful, but you will not like me. What am I?

89. I have one eye that I never close although I never use it to see. What am I?

90. What do you call someone who is afraid of Santa Claus?

91. Which is the hardest key to turn?

92. A young girl went home crying because, her boyfriend had just broken up with her. When she got home she broke her phone that had all their pictures together. What broke first?

93. This is something that you can never choose. However, you can always pick it. What is it?

94. What year will remain the same even when turned upside down?

95. You scream, I scream and we all scream. Why do we scream?

96. A farmer had 10 sheep, 10 pigs and 10 chickens. If we call the sheep pigs, how many pigs will there be?

97. I am covered with flowers, but I do not have soil. I have four legs, but I cannot walk. Three times a day I will hold your meals but, I never eat. What am I?

98. Why are teddy bears never hungry?

99. What did Tony the Tiger wear to bed?

100. What is the only thing that tastes better than it smells?

101. How can you tell apart a tree and a dog?

102. I was on the way to the movies when I passed an old man who had three sons. Each son also had a son. How many people went to the movies?

103. What instrument do skeletons play?

104. Sheila is turning 20 this year. However, she just turned 19 yesterday. How is this possible?

105. Why was the pirate always unable to finish the alphabet?

106. When am alive, you sing. When I die you clap your hands. What am I?

107. What state in the US is able to make the most writing utensils?

108. What do spiders like to eat along with their hamburgers?

109. Why was the car not feeling unwell?

110. I am always the one in charge and you will never find me in debt. Of all my relatives, I am known to be the first. You will find me in cars, but you will never find me in buses. They do not use me in Mexico, but they need me in Canada. What am I?

111. It is right when pronounced wrong and wrong when pronounced right. What is it?

112. You cannot find it in decades, years or days, but you will surely find it in seasons, seconds, centuries and minutes. What is it?

113. When am brand new, I am very relaxed, When they want to play with me, they stuff me. When you pinch me, I will

surely let out all my gas, but it does not have any smell. What am I?

114. It may seem easy, but very difficult for some people. You require some very good mental skills for you to know what it means and great imagination to understand and solve it. What is it?James and Zack made a bet before the beginning of a soccer game. James said the score before the game would be 0-0. Zack opposed, but eventually ended up losing. Why did Zack lose?

26

LOGIC RIDDLES

1. If you are alone in a dark room and you have a matchbox and a match, and then the only items you have in the room are a candle, firewood and an oil lamp, what would you light first?
2. I have married your friends, I married your aunts and uncles, I married your workmates. There is a probability that I married you too or soon I will. Who am I?
3. You and your friends went swimming and decided to compete. There are five of you and you are in the fourth place. Then, just before the end, you pass the third swimmer. What number are you now?
4. Jack is taller than John. Rebecca is taller than Ken. Sarah, on the other hand, is taller than Ken. Beverly is shorter than Rebecca and taller than Sara. How do you put the people in order from the tallest to the shortest?
5. You have a crate that can hold 19 shoes yet you have 304 pairs of shoes. How many crates do you need for all your shoes to fit in?
6. It took 4 men to build a house in 2 days. How long would it take 2 men to complete the same house?

7. I will always be covered in dirt and people will always step on me. However, whenever they are in trouble they will come running back to me. What am I?

8. Sheila and Shaila were born together simultaneously, but they are not the same age. Why are they not age mates?

9. I am usually warm but you can make me cold or hot. I am always running, but I can also be very calm. I can slip through anything, what am I?

10. You will often catch me swinging on sticks because that is where I do my tricks. I use white powder because it gives me a better grip and people will always applaud as they watch me. What am I?

11. It goes round and round every day, every hour and every minute. It will always stop from number to number just to hang out with them. What is it?

12. It has branches yet it does not have fruits, leaves or trunks. What is it?

13. Up and up it goes, but down it never goes. What is it?

14. What kind is a horse that has no body or legs? It jumps, but never runs?

15. It can fly and also crawl. It has two hands, one longer than the other, but it does not have wings or legs. What is it?

16. A parent looked at their child and said, "you're my son but am not your father." Who said this?

17. You have 10 yellow socks and 10 red socks in a bag. What is the least number of socks you need to take out of the bag so that you are left with a pair?

18. A horse was tied on its neck by a 10-meter rope. On the other hand, the hay stable is 20 meters away, but the horse was still able to access the hay. How did he manage to reach the stable?

19. You have an encyclopedia that has 10 books, which are carefully stored in a shelf. Each of the 10 books has 1.000pages. How many pages are there altogether between the first page and the last page without counting the covers?

20. You got sick and went to see the doctor who prescribed you some medications. He gave you three tablets that you are supposed to take within the space of thirty minutes. What would be the time difference between the first and last tablet?

21. Two daughters and two mothers are going to the salon, but in reality, only three went to the salon. How did this happen?

22. A cane has two ends. How many ends do 5 and a half canes have?

23. Mr Smith has two children. If the older child is a girl, what are the odds that the younger one is a girl?

24. When does homework stop being homework?

25. A young woman lost her mother to death. On the day of her mother's funeral, she met a handsome young man whom she immediately fell in love with. However, after the funeral, she went looking for the young man but could not find him. In frustration, she killed her sister. Why did she kill her own sister?

26. You want to give your friends a treat by taking them to the movies. How would you save more? Is it by taking one friend to the movies two times or by taking two friends to the movies at the same time?

27. There were four runners in a race. Dan finished the race before Allan, but Becca was not in the third place. Between Allan and Carlos, there were two runners. Who won first place in the race?

28. A group of friends were hanging out in the library after a group discussion. One of the friends then told his friends that he had just come across a hidden bill in one of the books. He said the $100 bill was between pages 34 and 35. However, none of his friends went to look for the money. Why did they not go?

29. You have two plastic jugs that are filled with water. If you wanted to put all this water into a barrel without using the jugs or any dividers and still tell which water is which, how would you do that?

30. What was there before was was was?

31. John and James are twins. One twin always tells the truth while the other twin is always lying about something. If you wanted to find out which twin is which, which yes or no question would you ask them to tell them apart?

32. An Uber driver was assigned the task of taking passengers to a train station, which normally takes an hour to get there. However, on that specific day, there was too much traffic that it took the Uber driver an hour and a half to get there. On his way back after dropping his passengers, the traffic was still heavy but this time it just took 90 minutes. How was that possible?

33. There were three adults in a park who were hanging out together. They were all struggling to get under one small umbrella and fortunately, none got wet. How did that happen?

34. There was a rabbit who was jumping towards a river. He came across 4 giraffes who saw 3 monkeys each. Each monkey had a parrot on its hands. What was the total number of animals who were going towards the river?

35. Mary's mother has four daughters. Kaka, Keke and Kiki. Who is the fourth daughter?

36. How long would it take you to finish reading a book if the book is a three hundred book, and you start reading it, then the next day you start reading half of the remaining book each day that follows?

37. Assuming that you were born in an odd year like 1993. Would you then celebrate your 50th birthday in an even year or an odd year?

38. Every second Sunday of May is Mother's day. That in mind, which would be the earliest possible date for these celebrations and which would be the latest date for the celebrations?

39. If someone says that everything they say is a lie, would that be a truth or a lie?

40. If three types of apples are mixed in a bowl, how many apples should you take to ensure that you end up with at least 2 apples for each type?

41. There was a man in a Library who was rushing out and he accidentally dropped his books down. 20 eyes stared at him because he was too loud. How many people were there in the library?

42. Jade is looking at Ann but Ann is looking at George. Jade is married but George is not. Is a married man looking at an unmarried person?

43. You are in a bathtub that gets full and you want to empty it. You have a spoon,
a cup and a bucket. Which would be the easiest way for you to empty the bathtub?

44. You are in a competition and then you overtake the last person. What are you now?

45. There are 15 apples on the table. I take 6 and you take 4 of the apples. How many apples do you have in total?

46. If you are in a queue and there are six of you, you are in the middle but then someone suggests that you have to

be arranged alphabetically. So, you take the position that number two had taken. What are you now?

27

EASY RIDDLES

1. My mother has 12 children. I am the second born and yet am the shortest. After every four years, I grow a little taller. Do you know me?
2. All the numbers had a fashion show and I carried the day. Who am I?
3. I am in everyone. From birth, you have me. But, if you do not want me, you can get rid of me. However, be sure I will soon be back. If you want me to be long, you just need to take care of me for some time and in no time I will be all grown.
4. I am a drink that people drink all over the world and adults say I help to keep them awake.
5. I am every child's favorite old man because I make their wishes come true.
6. I give taste to every meal you want to cook. Sometimes, you use a lot of me, but most times you need to use me in moderation.
7. What is the most genius insect that wins all the contests?
8. I am the bravest and the king of the jungle. My wife has beards and I do not.

9. Everyone keeps their treasure inside me. I am light and easily portable. Men keep me inside their trousers while women hide me inside their handbags.

10. It is the only number that stands straight and is always single even on valentines.

11. Where do the planets get rings from if they want to get married?

12. I am a fruit. If you carry me to a park with many monkeys, they will surely fight you.

13. We are siblings with the same mother and father. However, we have never shared any moments together.

14. I am very hard, but when you warm me I will cry and die.

15. I am a precious commodity, but I have no use when am still stored To see my value, you have to destroy me.

16. People see me and think they need to bathe or get wet if you are on the rains. However, with me, you will not be in any contact with the water.

17. Everyone has to go through this body process, which differentiates between adults and children. Many people want to reverse it, but they cannot.

18. You can keep all kinds of foods safe, cooked or uncooked. I will be warm on my outside, but very cold in my inside.

19. I am not hot, I am not sharp and I sure do not bite. However, you cannot hold me for more than some minutes longer.

20. You can only eat it at night, but never ever in the morning.

21. You cannot kill me by shooting me with a gun, nor can you destroy me by a sword. However, I only have two enemies who know my secret and they are gas and water.

22. I am the hardest tangible thing in your body. You can use me as a fighting tool if you are weak; however, you have to be careful because you can lose me.

23. You will only know if you are inside or outside by the side of me you are at.
24. I am good to smell, but if you put any edible on me, you will no longer want to eat it.
25. I am one, but when you add a letter to me, I will be gone. What do you need to add to me?
26. The whole of this is water, but it is mostly dry. What is it?
27. I am a digit. When you have just one of me, I am very valueless, but the more of me there is at the end of other digits, the wealthier and powerful you will be.
28. When you catch me, you will feel so weak and so uncomfortable. You will be stuck with me for some time if you do not see a specialist.
29. Everyone wants everyone free of any sickness, but if everyone is, I will suffer. Who am I?
30. A teacher's sister was involved in an accident and was badly injured. However, the injured did not have any sister. Can you help explain this?
31. Who shaves the most, but never goes bald?
32. Always happy when others marry and always finds people to marry, but has never married himself.
33. I look like a human. I have long hair, eyes, nose ears, legs, hands and mouth. However, I cannot talk, neither can I eat. Who am I?
34. I am very slow and shy. Most times you will catch me sleeping, but I will sneak out when I want to eat or drink. I can be very heavy especially if am very old.
35. You will never catch me on land alive; you cannot keep me as a pet because you like to eat me. I have 8 legs.
36. People cannot live without me, they say that I am life. You need me inside your body and outside your body as

well. Sometimes, you will play with me, but most times you want me safely stored and clean. Do you know me?

37. Teachers need me, students need me more. When they look at me, they can communicate even without talking. When I turn my color into white, I become unclean, but when I am black, I am very clean.

38. What is as big as you are, but you are heavier than it is?

39. You have parents whom you call mother and father, but they do not call you their daughter. Who are you?

40. My brother and I are always together. However, my brother is always making mistakes, which I always try my best to remove. What am I?

41. You will only know that am growing old by how shorter I get. I do not bend, but the shorter I get, the more I am getting close to death.

42. It is the lightest of them all, it has no smell and it is not tangible. Everyone has it. What is it?

43. They are twins and they work together every day. When one sleeps, they all sleep. When one is awake, they all wake up. However, they never talk and they meet. Who are they?

44. When a husband wants to surprise their wife, they will buy it. It is something women wear, but they need help to wear it. What is it?

45. When your plate is too hot, you will place it on top of it. It has legs, but whenever you want it to move, you have to push it. What is it?

46. It is a fruit you eat and looks like an orange, but it is not an orange. It is very sour, but it takes away your cold

47. You cannot see yourself, but through me, you will. I will copy everything you do and I will double everything you do.

48. If you are able to carry it, then you are not allowed to get inside it. However, if you are unable to carry it, you will always be inside. What is it?
49. If you try me, you will be arrested and jailed, but if you do me, you will not be jailed. Who am I?
50. Everyone has it and for everyone. It also increases after some months. However, it never decreases though everyone would want it less and less. What is it?
51. Your mother has three sons. Kenny, Chris and?
52. You bought me for breakfast, but you cannot drink me. What am I?
53. There was a very terrible road accident that left every single person dead. Who survived?
54. What is the total number of letters that you can find in the alphabet?
55. What is the only thing you can always count on?
56. You will always find it ahead, but you can never see it?
57. Which month do people eat the least food?
58. It moves every day and it does not get tired. But, if you do not change it after a while, it will sleep until you wake it up. What is it?
59. Some think that you can only drink water. I am water you can drink, but at times, you will be eating me. What kind of water am I?
60. Every home has this, it is something you need to use every day. You cannot eat it because it is not edible. Sometimes, it will be liquid and sometimes solid. You will use it by putting it on water and everything will be left sparkling clean. What is it?
61. What did Adam and Eve have as a desert when they went out for the first time?
62. What has branches, but no money is kept there?

63. It runs up and down and helps people move up and down easily. What is it?

64. I will never pant, but I am always going round and round, only going off once in a while.

65. Why do all celebrities never sweating, even when they keep performing?

66. It is a table that you cannot use to hold all your stuff safely.

67. How is it possible that you dropped an egg, but it did not break?

68. All the alphabets sat for an examination that they were all graded. Which letter was likely to outsmart the rest?

69. When you visit this place, you will get all sorts of stories and much more information that you may need. Which is this place?

70. I am something you wear only when it is very cold. You will only wear it on your hands, but you can eat and write while it is still on.

71. What is the only thing that should never go inside a cooking pot?

72. When you say its name, it sounds like its just one letter. However, if you want to write its name you need three letters to make sense out of it. It is the reason why you do not stumble on things and the reason why you iden-tify people and things. What is it?

73. The more you crack it, the happier you get. What is it?

74. People will look for different ways to lose it, it is uncom-fortable and people catch it unwillingly.

75. No one has ever seen it, but everyone is always looking forward to it. Once you reach it, it will always change its name. What is it?

28

ANSWERS FOR THANKSGIVING RIDDLES

1. Turkey
2. Potato
3. Corn
4. Pilgrims
5. Cranberry
6. Candied Yams
7. Football
8. Cornucopia
9. Mayflower
10. Pumpkin
11. A Turkey holding its breath.
12. Pie
13. Thanksgiving parade
14. Corn
15. The letter "I"
16. They used their foul language.
17. A thanksgiving breakfast and a Thanksgiving lunch.

18. They are all stuffed

19. The outer side.

20. A Turkey that has cranberry sauce.

21. The third foot grew.

22. The turkey is stuffed.

23. No battery can be used since it is an electric cutter.

24. A Turkey used for Thanksgiving.

25. The part that has not been eaten.

26. The Thanksgiving host.

27. The turkey, ostriches do not fly.

28. Their Feet.

29. A Turkey that is praying so that it is not eaten.

30. You are so lucky to be eaten on only one special holiday. For me, this is the second time in one month.

31. Stuffed

32. Pilgrims

33. The Pilgrims

34. A wishbone

35. A banana

36. You put two scoops of ice cream, a pie and rubber, and then a turkey in a glass.

37. A dressed Turkey

38. A turkey

39. It had a fowl attitude

40. Squash

41. A gobbling banana

42. Zero hours because the turkey has already been roasted.

43. Sixteen pies

44. There was a very foul play that ended up in him dying.

45. The male turkey should have a beer belly.

46. A blushing turkey

47. A pie

48. In the Alphabets

49. Google! Google! Google!
50. Apples because the rest are all root vegetables.
51. Pilgrims
52. A turkey
53. Thanksgiving
54. Turkey
55. A stuffed roasted turkey
56. A turkey that is in an elevator
57. A pool-tree
58. A pumpkin
59. Foul Weather
60. Pumpkin Pi

29

ANSWERS FOR CUTE RIDDLES

1. Butterfly
2. Barbie doll
3. A teddy bear
4. Honey bees
5. A monkey
6. Funny
7. Burple
8. A cat
9. Sloths
10. A doll
11. Zebra
12. Ostrich
13. A unicorn
14. "ELEP" and "HANT"
15. A dog
16. Orchids
17. Cupids
18. Chocolates
19. Jewels

20. Make-up
21. It never rained
22. An engagement or a wedding ring
23. They are romantic comedies
24. Your girlfriend or girlfriend
25. A heart
26. A kiss
27. A date
28. Roses
29. Lips
30. A relationship
31. Boyfriends and husbands
32. A cupid covered with kisses
33. The heart
34. Super Mario
35. You are!
36. Tulip flowers
37. A heart

30

ANSWERS FOR CHRISTMAS RIDDLES

1. Christmas lights.
2. The 12 days of Christmas song
3. A Christmas tree
4. Christmas stockings
5. Jungle bells.
6. Why do you always hang around? Are you never tired?
7. It was already stuffed
8. A candy cane
9. A pineapple
10. A snow cone
11. The letter 'S'
12. Eggnog
13. Santa Claus in a laundry dryer
14. A frost bite
15. In a snowbank
16. If this medication does not make you better, ring me!
17. You get a turtle dove
18. Yule Tide detergent
19. They felt very shaken

20. Rude-dolf
21. The chicken had its own drum sticks
22. He gets snowflakes
23. In the north pool(north pole)
24. A wreath
25. There is a christmess
26. Claustrophobia
27. Its because Santa only visits once every year
28. They can sense his gifts
29. She gave the snowman a cold shoulder
30. St. Nickle-less (Nicholus)
31. Because of the nut cracker
32. It does not matter the name you call him because he won't hear you either way since he has the earmuffs on.
33. The snow cone
34. The Christmas stockings
35. Hi gorgeous!
36. The English alphabet is different because it does not have the EL
37. They are called relative clauses
38. A spanking
39. Mini-vans
40. A missile toe
41. The sleigh was in the house
42. A pole-aroid camera
43. A humbug
44. To learn the elf-abets
45. Snowflakes
46. Santa Jaws
47. They used the hairdryer
48. A puddle
49. A stocking
50. A fleece navidad

51. A subordinate clause
52. A silent night
53. He did not have legs
54. You would get a crisp kringle
55. Tinsilitis
56. Because they like all the wrappings
57. In the claus-et (closet)
58. Because he owns a black belt
59. Nothing because the reindeers do not talk
60. Frosted flakes
61. Santa pause
62. North polish
63. Santa claws
64. Jungle bells! Jungle bells! Jungle bells!
65. They were afraid of Santa Claws
66. A Christmas tree
67. Reindeer
68. A candy cane
69. A Christmas stocking
70. An elf
71. Mistletoe
72. Santa Claus
73. Christmas lights
74. Christmas wreath
75. Nativity scene
76. Snow
77. Advent calendar
78. The turkey because he is stuffed
79. Cupid
80. Comet
81. It is Christmas Eve!
82. Because they are always dropping needles
83. Dasher

84. A broken drum because you just can't beat it!
85. The South Pole. From the North Pole there is no other direction that you can take
86. Every year because every year there's a Christmas day and every year there is a new year's day.
87. He has Santa claws
88. Platform shoes

31

ANSWERS FOR WINTER RIDDLES

1. Snow
2. Gloves
3. Penguins
4. Sled
5. Skis
6. A coat
7. Icicle
8. Snow angel
9. Scarf
10. Christmas trees
11. Fireplace
12. Snowman
13. Thermometer
14. Ice
15. Eskimos
16. A wreath
17. Winter
18. Snow because they are ice crystals
19. They are all very cold

20. Winter gloves
21. A dreidel
22. A shovel
23. Blizzard
24. The letter 'R'
25. Snow white
26. Winter Olympics games
27. An Avalanche
28. Poinsettia
29. Royal Penguin
30. The arctic
31. Snow
32. An apple
33. Skis
34. Sled
35. Snowman
36. Winter coats
37. A Christmas tree
38. Rudolf the red nosed reindeer
39. Christmas stockings
40. Chimney
41. Snowball
42. Chocolate
43. A snow
44. They all have temperature
45. Hanukkah
46. Icicle
47. Snowman
48. Frostbite
49. A fireplace
50. Hot chocolate
51. Snow
52. They were making snow angels.

53. Decemberrrr
54. A north pole
55. An ice-burgler
56. Because the wind went through their bones
57. During the snowball
58. Brrrr-itos
59. Water
60. An icecap
61. An iceberger
62. A snowball
63. A snowball
64. They sit by the fireplace and warm themselves
65. Frosted flakes
66. They melt
67. Brrr-d
68. Because they could not walk
69. Snowman
70. Winter
71. Because Frost bites
72. A fireplace
73. A polar bear

32

ANSWERS FOR HALLOWEEN RIDDLES

1. A spider
2. A ghost
3. Witches
4. Blood
5. Bats
6. Mr Skeleton
7. Vampires
8. The mummy
9. A werewolf
10. Bones
11. Frankenstein's monster
12. A pumpkin
13. A broomstick
14. A coffin
15. Cauldron
16. The haunted house
17. A black cat
18. A tombstone
19. The living room

20. C and Y c(and)y
21. The dead-end
22. When you are a mouse
23. They heard that a cereal killer was on the loose
24. She was too wrapped in herself
25. An ice scream
26. He was allergic to nuts
27. In the claws-it
28. Use a pumpkin patch
29. Mas-scare-a
30. The web is the trick and you are obviously the treat
31. He wanted to be taught how to draw blood
32. The ghost is invisible
33. They are left in day care
34. You get a cold spell
35. Sherlock bones
36. Trombone
37. Boo berries
38. They loved to Boogie
39. A broom with a view
40. Hi Boo?
41. Lazybones
42. His haunting license had long expired
43. To let the witch hikers pass through
44. So that they can read all the horoscopes
45. Rhythm and boos
46. A Skeleton
47. A mummy
48. A coffin
49. A funny bone
50. Ghosts
51. A black cat
52. The Dead Sea

53. A bat in a batmobile
54. Blood
55. A fence
56. You get blood tests
57. A ghost in an elevator
58. They always take a coffin break
59. A bloodhound
60. A bright Jack O'lantern
61. Snow white's Apple
62. Santa Claus
63. A cemetery
64. A light ale
65. Donald Trump dressed as a witch
66. It is a pumpkin pie!
67. You can never tell the difference because they are twin witches
68. An elephant that is riding on a witch's broomstick
69. All witches are ugly
70. A candy
71. The devil
72. No-body
73. At the ghost office
74. The letter 'I'
75. Bats
76. Treats
77. Prank-kenstien
78. Halloween
79. Hollow-ween
80. An Apple
81. A pumpkin

33

ANSWERS FOR SHORT RIDDLES

1. A Mongoose
2. A towel
3. A telephone
4. Wrong
5. A pineapple
6. A gift
7. A needle
8. She is at an eye glass store
9. The name of the horse was Friday
10. Tuesday paid the bill, he was the third friend.
11. Farts
12. They both need a beating
13. Life
14. You can use all the apples to make an apple sauce which everyone will have.
15. A bill
16. Shoes because you get to remove them at night.
17. A fish when it goes in and out of water.
18. A blade of grass

19. An upright piano

20. Sea urchins

21. A top

22. The lungs

23. They both want to be bailed out

24. Heaven

25. A puppy

26. Money

27. Feathers because bird need them to fly and elderly men used it to write as a Quill pen.

28. When it strikes one

29. Parents

30. Because they had racquets

31. He did not fall on the ground. He fell on top of 30 people.

32. Zero because they all ran away once they heard him approach

33. A cell out (sell-out)

34. A kit-ty carson

35. Because it was turned on

36. Fire

37. A matchstick

38. A sign

39. Hell-o (hello)

40. a wedding ring

41. A comb

42. They both take a long time to leave

43. Arrrgh

44. A bat

45. They are all girls

46. When he gets rattled

47. Blood money

48. A dormouse

49. Hungary

50. Room for improvement
51. A full moon
52. A fly
53. A clock
54. Small
55. A bottle
56. Because his batteries died
57. The letter C
58. The post office
59. An egg
60. Because he's still living and not dead
61. A teapot
62. Every month has 28 days
63. He was bald
64. Eleven(the alphabet)
65. In the dictionary
66. A relationship
67. Ann is the fifth daughter
68. The letter M
69. Silence
70. A palm
71. There will be no smoke since it is an electric train
72. The stars
73. Because they cannot cook
74. Age
75. Your feet off the floor
76. It would become wet
77. A table
78. Add G and its 'gone'
79. No one because the coconut tree does not have bananas
80. They are both in the middle of the water
81. Yesterday, Today and Tomorrow
82. Stinker ball

83. The word incorrectly
84. Because they are always stuffed
85. Yolk book
86. You should go bald
87. Because fingers are supposed to be in both hands not one hand
88. Long time, no sea
89. The one who has the biggest head
90. 12 months
91. They use hare planes
92. River bank
93. A telephone
94. Breakfast and lunch
95. A cup cake
96. He wanted to have sweet dreams
97. Smiles because there is a mile between S and s
98. They both weigh the same.
99. The president lives in the white house
100. The road
101. Yesterday
102. Nine
103. Letter 'v'
104. The one with the biggest head
105. A mushroom
106. Adam because he was the first in the human race.
107. Your name
108. A sponge
109. You can never find dry stones
110. A keyboard
111. They were a granddad, dad and grandson
112. A human being. You crawl as a baby (4 legs) walk as an adult (2 legs) and use a cane when you get old(3 legs)
113. A breath

114. The word wrong

115. A mirror

116. The street

117. A river

118. A battery

119. A map

120. A doorbell

121. A candle

122. Tomorrow

123. A piano

124. Water

125. Nothing

126. Fire

127. Footsteps

128. A plate

129. A coffin

130. An umbrella

131. A promise

132. A Candle

133. An egg

134. Fire

135. A pillow

136. A corn on a cob. You throw the husk, cook and eat the kernels then throw away the cob

137. The moon

138. An echo

139. A hole

140. A secret

141. A cold

142. An egg

143. Rain

144. A tree

145. An address

146. An alphabet
147. A flag
148. Stairs
149. A Tree
150. Trouble
151. A bottle
152. Kittens
153. A horse
154. The shadow of an elephant
155. As fur as possible
156. A rhinoceros
157. Monkeys and donkeys

34

ANSWERS FOR WHO AM I RIDDLES

1. Their daughter
2. Letter R
3. Woman, Oman and man
4. a Lifeguard
5. A dentist
6. The sun
7. The heart
8. A ball
9. A baby
10. Tree
11. A flower
12. A balloon
13. A television
14. Shoes
15. A coat
16. Ice cream
17. Eyeball
18. A milk truck
19. A frog

20. A bar of soap
21. Gloves
22. A cloud
23. A kangaroo
24. A coin
25. A doughnut
26. Light switch
27. Strawberry
28. A rooster
29. A peacock
30. Halloween
31. A peach
32. A library
33. Capital letters
34. An aluminium foil
35. First base
36. An Easter Bunny
37. A ghost
38. An anchor
39. A banana
40. Cheeks
41. Santa Claus
42. A nest
43. A farm
44. An island
45. A rainbow
46. A catfish
47. A carrot
48. A bulldog
49. An onion
50. A plane
51. A tree
52. The moon

53. The stars

54. An aeroplane

55. A kite

56. A cell phone

57. Ohio

58. Letter 'O'

59. Hair

60. Darkness

61. Silence

62. Ice

63. The brain

64. A potato

65. An egg

66. Traffic lights

67. Money

68. A bat

69. An onion

70. A dream

71. A window

72. An orange

73. An x-ray

74. A neck

75. A calendar

76. Light

77. A temperature

78. A finger

79. A mop

80. Breath

81. A joke

82. A Teabag

83. Swims

35

ANSWERS FOR FUNNY RIDDLES

1. Letter 'C'
2. Letter 'W'
3. It was a one storey
4. Two because she only took two.
5. Racecar backwards
6. You had thrown it high in the sky.
7. Seven. You take S and it will become Even.
8. He fell off the bottom step.
9. Right between the eyes.
10. Stop imagining
11. You should just open the fridge and let the elephant go in because the fridge might be the size of the elephant.
12. You let the elephant out and then let the giraffe go in.
13. The giraffe did not attend the meeting since he was inside the fridge.
14. You should just cross the river since all the animals including the crocodiles are in the meeting.
15. You should put the money in front of a mirror
16. A shadow

17. Its 'AND'
18. Silence
19. Because you only stop looking once you find what you were looking for.
20. He sleeps at night.
21. Second place
22. Because they hunt knights
23. Thunder
24. Leapfrog
25. Cricket
26. Letter 'R'
27. The future
28. In the dictionary
29. A piano
30. Blue paint
31. Bookkeeper
32. Penal-tea
33. Water
34. An anchor
35. Because he had just one pupil.
36. They're all beds
37. Your laps
38. They get toad
39. It uses a rain check
40. The library
41. Because she wanted to rock and roll
42. Beef jerky
43. Sherlock bones
44. An investigator
45. Catch you later
46. Your right arm or elbow
47. Ton
48. A towel

49. Queue
50. Your eyes
51. The door
52. He was walking and not driving.
53. None because it wasn't Moses but Noah who went inside
    the ark
54. Hey! I just had a bright idea.
55. In the flea market
56. A milkshake
57. A newspaper
58. A moo-tel
59. HISStory
60. Greece
61. It concentrates
62. A shadow
63. Because Thanksgiving was right at the corner
64. For beating the eggs
65. Because his feet stink
66. A blind man
67. He tasted funny
68. Mississippi
69. Because she was all wrapped up
70. He did not have guts
71. In their bloody mobiles
72. A wrap song
73. Because they are a bunch of nobodies
74. Twig or treat
75. At the spooky post office
76. Dead ends
77. They are meewsical
78. A haunted doll house
79. By a witch watch
80. You cannot lie to me, I can see right through you

81. At the dead sea
82. On fry-days
83. See you next month
84. Broom-mates
85. He had nobody
86. Turn on the dark am afraid of the light
87. So they can know which witch is which
88. A toilet
89. Hilarious
90. They plan-et
91. Poop
92. Facebook
93. Weewee
94. I have so many problems
95. Just one. Second February
96. You can't see me.
97. Vegetables
98. You pay for electricity
99. Who knows
100. Letter 'N'
101. Pea
102. Black
103. Your shadow
104. Nothing, they just waved at each other.
105. Move from one spot to another
106. When you are eating a watermelon
107. Paper

36

ANSWERS FOR MATH RIDDLES

1. Three because the grandfather is also a father. The father is also a son.
2. Zero because roosters do not lay eggs.
3. Seven because he broke every egg but seven were not touched
4. The house is already built so you do not need any men to work on it.
5. Zero
6. The score is always 0-0 before the game begins
7. Because it's time. Its 9 am and when you add 5 hours to it, you will be at 2 pm.
8. It could be either of these three answers. 51 and 15, 42 and 24 and 60 and 06
9. He only has 3 dogs. One dog is corgi, another one a pug and lastly a lab.
10. 25 years old
11. A decimal is what should be added. 5.6 is bigger than 5 but 5.6 is lesser than 6
12. The notebook costs $120 and the pen costs $20

13. Halfway because after that, the cat will be running out of the forest.
14. Once because once you remove 5 it is no longer 25 but 20.
15. Do you want to hear my problems?
16. One has 3 letters, three has 5 letters and five has 4 letters. Four, on the other hand, has 4 letters. Most of the numbers will always come back to the magical number 4.
17. 888+88+8+8+8=1000
18. Sea-plus
19. Because you can use your cow-culator
20. Pi
21. It grew square roots
22. Multi-pliers
23. Alge-bros

37

ANSWERS FOR TRICKY RIDDLES

1. Fish and ships
2. A sourpuss
3. Because every lunch went for seconds
4. He wasn't peeling well
5. He was two tired(too tired)
6. Car tunes
7. He was feeling crummy
8. Because it was a better batter
9. Hot air baboons
10. He split
11. You put holes in it
12. One watches cells while the other sells watches
13. A goose
14. It became a wet white shirt
15. Because pepper water makes them sneeze
16. Because there are too many cheetahs (cheaters)
17. A fruit fly
18. They chase after parked cars
19. Wednesday who was the third friend did.

20. Money
21. The hospital room, which he was born at was 1990 and the hospital room he died at was 1964
22. The Amazon because it still existed even before it was discovered.
23. A bar of gold
24. There is no man who has 5 heads
25. An e-cigarette does not produce any smoke
26. A teapot
27. Eyes
28. You just draw a shorter line next to the line and that will make your line longer.
29. It has a hole in it
30. A kiwi
31. Fire
32. A flag
33. A pillow
34. D-A-Y
35. Rain
36. A tree
37. 16 cars
38. Sunday
39. 12
40. None because they both weigh one kilogram
41. A bed
42. Breakfast
43. A tennis ball
44. Later
45. Because monkeys copy everything they see
46. Because he is blind
47. Because 7 ate (8) 9
48. A needle
49. Your hair

50. A dead person
51. A screw driver
52. Liquid, solid, gas
53. A yardstick
54. Just one because after you put one book. The bag is no longer empty.
55. A keyhole
56. Rabies
57. A mirror
58. A hole
59. A clock
60. An umbrella
61. The smoke
62. A secret
63. Ten-ish
64. Your eyes
65. Cupid
66. A porcupine
67. The car door
68. A fence
69. Rinda, Jack, Max, John and Linda
70. Two. The inside and the outside
71. A doorbell
72. A mongoose
73. A road
74. Letter 'g'
75. A garbage truck
76. He neverlands
77. He weighs meat
78. The students were bright
79. The wind
80. Are you asleep? Because you are already sleeping
81. They will put it under the g'rilla

82. Your nose

83. He wanted to go to a high school

84. Your shadow

85. He was only on the first step

86. Darkness

87. Nept-tune

88. A fart

89. A needle

90. Claus-trophobic

91. A don-key

92. Her heart because her boyfriend had broken it first

93. Your nose

94. 1961

95. For ice cream

96. 10 because calling the sheep pigs does not make them pigs.

97. A table

98. They are always stuffed

99. Paw-jamas

100. The tongue

101. By their bark

102. Just one, you because everyone else was passing

103. Trombones

104. His birthday is on 31st December and the said day is 1st January which makes it a totally new year

105. He always got lost at sea

106. A birthday candle

107. Pencil-vania

108. French flies

109. He had gas

110. Letter 'a'

111. The word wrong

112. Letter 'n'

113. A balloon

114. A riddle

115. Because James was right. Before every game starts the score is always at 0-0

38

ANSWERS FOR LOGIC RIDDLES

1. The match because you need to see through the dark-room.
2. A priest
3. Third place
4. Rebecca, Beverly, Sara, Jack and John
5. 304 pairs total to 608 single shoes. So, 608/19=32
6. The house is already built so you do not need any men to build the house again.
7. A baseball base
8. There were both born at the same moment but due to time differences, they were born on different dates.
9. Water
10. A gymnast
11. A clock
12. A bank
13. A person's age
14. A chess piece
15. Time
16. The mother

17. Two, because you have not been told the socks have to be of the same color

18. The other end was not tied to anything

19. 8.000pgs.

20. One hour

21. They are grandmother, mother and daughter

22. 12 ends

23. 50 per cent

24. When you hand it over to the teacher

25. She killed her sister because she was hoping that the man who was at her mother's funeral would show up at her sister's.

26. You would save more by taking two friends to the movies at the same time because then, you would only buy 3 tickets. However, if you took just one friend then you would buy a total of four tickets

27. Carlos won. There were two runners between Allan and Carlos who is either 1st or 4th positions which would go to either Carlos or Allan. Becca and Dan are either in the 2nd or 3rd position. Becca wasn't 3rd Dan has to be 3rd and Becca 2nd. Since Dan finished before Allan that means Allan was 4th and Carlos was 1st.

28. Because the odd number in a book is always on the right while the even page number is always on the left. Therefore, the page numbers are not facing each other, thus no money can be hidden there.

29. You can freeze one or both jugs, then cut the plastic and only leave the ice. After that, you can put the jugs in a barrel and you will be able to tell which water came from which bag.

30. The answer is 'IS'. The question is asking the verb that was there before was became past tense.

31. You should ask them either of the two questions:
    (a) If their brother would tell the truth
    (b) If they are twins
    The twin that tells the truth will answer yes to both questions while the twin that lies will answer no to both questions.
32. One and a half hours is the same as 90 minutes.
33. It is not raining and that's why they were not rained on.
34. Just one, the rabbit. The other animals were just passing
35. Mary
36. You would never finish it because you will only be reading half of what was previously left.
37. In an odd year. This is because the first celebration was in an even year and, therefore, the sequence is 1st year (even), 2nd year (odd), 3rd year (odd) etc.
38. The earliest would be May 8th and the latest would be May 14th
39. A lie since the statement itself says everything is a lie.
40. 4 apples. There are 3 types of apples if you take 4 that will give you 2 apples for each type.
41. 11 people. 20 eyes mean there are 10 people in the room plus the man himself.
42. Yes because if Ann is married, she is looking at George who is unmarried. If Ann is not married, then jade is looking at the unmarried woman.
43. Pull off the plug.
44. You cannot overtake the last person in a race. The only person you can overtake is the one in front of you.
45. Four since you only took four
46. Second.

39

ANSWERS FOR EASY RIDDLES

1. February
2. Number 8
3. Hair
4. Coffee
5. Santa Claus
6. Oil
7. The spelling bee
8. The lion
9. A wallet
10. No one
11. Saturn because he has many rings
12. A banana
13. Night and day
14. Ice cubes
15. An egg
16. A baby shower
17. Ageing
18. A fridge
19. Breath

20. Dinner
21. Fire
22. Teeth
23. Door
24. A nose
25. Letter 'G'
26. A cloud
27. Zero
28. A cold
29. A doctor
30. The teacher is the brother
31. A barber shaving his clients
32. A priest
33. A doll
34. A turtle
35. An octopus
36. Water
37. A blackboard
38. Your shadow
39. Their son
40. An eraser
41. A pencil
42. Your breath
43. Eyes
44. A necklace
45. A table
46. A lemon
47. A mirror
48. A coffin
49. Suicide
50. Age
51. You
52. A cup / Thermos

53. All the people who were couples
54. T-H-E-A-L-P-H-A-B-E-T
55. Your fingers
56. The future
57. February because it is the only month with the least number of days
58. A clock
59. Watermelon
60. Soap
61. Apples
62. A tree
63. Stairs
64. A clock
65. Because they have many fans
66. A periodic table
67. It was already boiled
68. Letter A because it is used to show the top grade
69. A library
70. A pair of gloves
71. Its lid
72. An eye
73. A joke
74. A cold
75. Tomorrow

4

BONUS

40

HOW TO WRITE A GOOD RIDDLE

1. Find What You Want to Talk About

A good riddle starts with finding what you like and what you want to talk about. That's easy for most of us. You can talk about anything or anyone. Do you like soccer? Then you can make your riddle about a soccer ball, a goalkeeper, the referee, or even the soccer field. Do you like singing? Then you can make your riddle about music, singers, songs or even musical instruments.

Do you like math? Then you'll be surprised to know that most of the riddles you'll find are math riddles. This shouldn't come as a surprise since numbers are found everywhere, from the time you leave school to the number of slices of pizza you eat on weekends. Many of the riddles you've read here are related to math in one way or another.

Have you found what you want to talk about? If not, you can ask for help. Ask a teacher, a friend, or a parent about something you like. It doesn't have to be something very elaborate. Just remember that the purpose of a riddle is to find the thing the riddle is about.

After thinking about the things, you want to talk about, try to describe it. Can you do so? Is the object round? Is it long? Is it something everybody has owned once? Is it something very common where you live? Is something only young or old people would be able to relate to? Do you know if it's something that won't hurt anyone's sensibilities?

2 Decide How you Want to Write it

After deciding what you want to talk about, you can think now of how you want to phrase your riddle. This is when you need to think a lot. There are many ways to write a riddle. Let's take a look at some examples:

You can write a **one-line riddle**. What is it? As its name tells us, a one-line riddle is a simple, easy-to-write riddle. It's very simple because you just have to write one or sometimes two lines to convey the riddle. Many things can be described using just a few words. Those few words can be used to make up a one-line riddle.

How can you phrase a one-line riddle? Most of the time, one-line riddles are phrased as questions. Some of them begin like this:

- What is red, blue, and grows on trees?
- Who screams at night and sleeps at night?
- What has one tail that never stops growing?

Other one-line riddles can be phrased as simple sentences. But even when then, they are followed by a simple question. Take a look at these:

- My mom didn't enough to buy a purse, but she took it anyway. How did she do it?
- Shan got lost in a very large city, but he found his way back home by looking at a horse, pig and apple. How did he do it?
- You can write to me, but I can write to you, too. What am I?

Some of these one-line riddles might sound like puns, and some of them are actually puns in themselves.

You can also write a **short riddle.** As its name tells us, they are rather short. How short? That depends on how you want to phrase it. Some of them can be written in just three or four lines. Most are made in a way that rhyme or with very few words. Of course, most of them also have a question at the end. Let's see some examples of these:

- I have three brothers but no sisters

I have 2 parents but no grandparents
I have many friends but no relatives,
How am I?

- It grows on trees from summer to summer

It walks on the ground from winter to winter
But it falls only in spring,
What is it?

· There were two men in my house

There are now two women and a mouse
There used to be no one in this house,
Who's really inside my house?

You can write a **long riddle** when you want to tell a story that has a surprising end or when you want to hide the answer so carefully that it might take a while for the person to decipher it.

A long riddle can be phrased as a story. These stories are long because they have a lot of details, and these are necessary to find the answer to the riddle. interestingly, many of these details, even though are many or subtle, can be found and remembered easily. They are in the riddle in a way that the person who tries to decipher it can never tell that he was being lied to or that the other person was trying to prank him or take advantage of him.

Many riddles are also long because, as stories, they entertain and being long help them to be fun to everyone. What you need to understand about them is that you can change anything about them: the names, number of people, objects, setting, and more. But the details that help decipher the riddle might be impossible to change.

You also need to have in mind that some riddles might not work very well in some cultures. This is obvious when you talk about money, places, countries, and even names. US dollars are not used in Russia, and the way Australians measure distance is not the same as in the United States.

History can also play a part in it. You'd be surprised to know that many nations don't have a history of participating in wars and so, talking about wars, veterans and things related to them would flat. In those cases, you can talk about nature or people since those are topics that almost everyone can relate to. Animals are also a safe bet.

Sometimes these differences can lend themselves to riddles. So don't be afraid to incorporate them into your riddles. Just think about the best way they can appear in your riddle. Be careful; don't employ prejudice, intolerance, lack of respect or racism in your riddle. These will prove to be of a very poor taste and might even get you into trouble.

3. Think About Your Audience

What's an audience? Simply put, an audience is everyone who listens to you. It doesn't matter if they're young or old, men or women, they're your audience if they are listening to your riddle and you're expecting them to solve it.

Thinking about your audience will help you determine the amount of details and choose which ones you will choose. If your audience is your classmates, then you might need to adapt your riddle in a way that your classmates will readily understand. You might not use a lot of difficult words or elaborate terms. You might not use things that they may have possibly never seen or heard.

Does your audience watch TV? Many do, but don't come to think that everyone likes the same things as you do. So, you might need to ask first if you want to use some TV references.

Does your audience like to play sports? Then, you might need to use sports references if you want them to understand your riddle. In other words, build your riddle as simple as possible for everyone to understand. Be flexible so that everyone can get them, too.

There are, of course, so many simple riddles that don't even need to change any detail because literally, everyone can solve them. Animals, fruits, vegetables, food, money, nature, and more will never fail to entertain. Sports, music, musical instrument, math, language, names of places, TV shows, gardening, cars and more might need a little explaining if you want your riddle to succeed.

4. Decide if you Want to Give Clues

In this book, you've seen many riddles. The great majority of them don't need clues to understand. Few of them have clues, either in the riddles themselves or in the answers.

Clues can be given at any time. If you're writing a long riddle, some details might count as clues. These clues can easily give away the answer to the riddle, so you have to find a way how they can be "hidden" or "camouflaged" so subtlely that they can be found but not so obvious that they give away the answer.

If you're writing a short riddle or a one-line riddle, then it might be pretty difficult to give as many clues as you want aside from the details you've already given. In such cases, you can give clues after you've told the riddle. You don't need to do this immediately after you've told the riddle; you can wait for your audience to try to decipher your riddle. If they seem to have a lot of difficulties understanding or solving it, then you might consider giving them some clues.

Clues can be many, or a few can be long or short. Just remember that an explanation is not a clue, but actually, an obvious description of the answer to the riddle.

5. Explain your Riddle

This, of course, doesn't need to be done all the time. This will depend a lot on your audience. If your audience can decipher the riddle easily, then you might not even need to explain it at all. So, when should you explain your riddle?

Some riddles are very difficult to solve. In those cases, after solving it, you might need to explain it as much as your audience needs. This is seen in math riddles and also in riddles that include a lot of details or unknown facts.

One clue to know whether your audience has understood your riddle or not is by noticing how they reacted to it. Did they make a gesture of surprise or disbelief? Did they look that they didn't get it? If so, you can explain the answer to your riddle and then make them realize how they could've gotten the same answer if they had paid attention to certain details.

Also, have in mind that most people don't like to show that they are embarrassed and so they won't tell you or even show that they didn't get the answer. They might want to know how you got the answer to the riddle but are not bold enough to ask for your reasoning.

Some riddles can be very hard, some can be very easy, some can be very long or others short, but all of them have the same purpose: to "conceal" and try to get the person to use their abilities and knowledge to guess what the riddle is about. Remember that there aren't impossible riddles, so don't worry if you ever come across if you ever encounter a difficult one. Chances are, you'll find the answer in the details.

41

CONCLUSION

A math book, a person, and this book. They all have something in common. What's that? They are all full of problems and funny moments. Those problems and funny moments have been employed in this book to find the best riddles. The problems make you think and the fun moments make you laugh and keep you reading and entertained.

In *Riddles for Smart Kids*, you have seen the best collection of riddles you can find. All of these original riddles were written in a way that kids can readily understand. Kids ages 4-12 are naturally curious and these riddles fulfill their natural appeal for solving problems on their own. *Riddles for Smart Kids* have shown a way for kids to think outside the box.

That was, and still is, the purpose of riddled and this book. More than just entertaining, they can also help everyone, especially children, think outside the box. In a world where books don't encourage people to think critically, a book of riddles can help kids do just that, helping them get out of their comfort zone. These riddles help them to pay attention to subtleties and details in a way they never thought they would.

Of course, we can't forget how entertaining they are. That's what endears them to many people. Riddles can be very personal as they can get. They are fun because the details are fun, the way a person tells it is fun and the surprise you can see on someone's face when he discovers the answer is so priceless that it actually is fun. The riddles you have seen in this book accomplish just that. Fun moments for kids and adults alike, and moments of surprise you will hardly forget.

Riddles for Smart Kids is the book you were wishing to have in your hands if you really wanted to entertain in a healthy, educational way. Never forget that riddles can be found and made anywhere and everywhere, but it takes one witty mind to solve them. What's more, it takes one wittier mind to build one, understand it, relate it and explain it in a way that's fun, curious and unforgettable.